LIFE
AFTER
THE
WIFE

LIFE
AFTER
THE
WIFE

Dave Pinder

authorHOUSE®

AuthorHouse™
1663 Liberty Drive
Bloomington, IN 47403
www.authorhouse.com
Phone: 1-800-839-8640

Published by AuthorHouse   08/21/2012

ISBN: 978-1-4772-2331-4 (sc)
ISBN: 978-1-4772-2333-8 (hc)
ISBN: 978-1-4772-2332-1 (e)

Dave. Yep that's me; "good old **Dave**" dependable, reliable, easy going, generous, funny, intelligent (well sort of; I have my moments) considerate, argumentative, perfect!!! Lol! Broadminded (very, as you will see) athletic!!! Sporty!!! Yep, I go to the gym probably not as much as I say I do lol but I go, look good in or out of my clothes and this bit is important—"beauty is in the eye of the beholder". Also remember this; "confidence cancels out beauty". That's a little lie but the truth is "it helps" big time.

Here's a little bit of background about me so you can get an idea of why I am who I am.

Not a happy childhood. Father in the services and strict and mother working long hours to pay the bills and my brother, sister and I are left to our own devices on many occasions. Little money, less than other kids my age but still more than some, good boxer as a kid, very mature could paint and decorate by the time I was 12, grew food in the garden and hardly went to school. I won't tell you in depth as I don't want the print to run off the page with your tears. But it was neither the easiest nor the hardest childhood. Left school and worked at a whole host of different jobs, fishing trawlers, farmhand, tyre fitter and apprentice mechanic. Apprentice store man, apprentice ladies hairdresser (okay, stop giggling, fella's, it helped me in later life, lol,) timber yard. I know what you're thinking and yep you're right, I never completed any opportunity I was given. I Joined the Army at eighteen and served nine years. Ran a driving school for eight years and worked for a blue chip company for twenty years. Took redundancy and my salary-based pension at the tender age of fifty two, did some little jobs like parcel delivery, cleaning, laminating, and then cleaning again. Oh and yeah, I was married TWICE; once at twenty for thirteen years, had two boys, then married for the second time for nineteen years and had one boy.

Father did time at Her Majesty's pleasure for seven years, mother stood by him, now they are living away from the family. One of my son's spent time inside for GBH and also at a rehab facility for heroin addiction.

As you can imagine I have gained many life skills during my interesting time as a child, teenager, young man, and a working adult and as well as being mechanically minded I am also very good at DIY and can do most of the building skills, including plumbing in bathrooms, fitting kitchens, tiling floors and walls, building patios and erecting fences.

I have lived in Malta, Cyprus, Germany, and visited Canada, USA, and most of Europe on holidays and /or with the Army.

I will say this; my marriage was over a long time before I left my first wife, and I was unfaithful to her with my second wife to be, but I was 100% faithful to my second wife.

Treated my second wife who was 16 years my junior like a queen (her words) I put everything into my marriage, lived for our family unit, then out of the blue, only three weeks after moving into the bungalow I now live in with my youngest son, my wife informed me that she did not love me anymore and that she had known this for at least 18 months.

What does that feel like? Well it's like the death of a close relative, like the worst news you could ever want to hear. Your gut turns over and you find emotions you never knew you had, your mind works overtime about how it's come to this and about what's going to happen next, weeks fly by, moods change, you think about all you've done together as a family, all the material things you have built together as a family. Reality hits home and you either hide or come out fighting; not in the real sense of the word, though you feel like you could whack!!! the bitch at times lol.

So what's your first move? A very good friend said to me, and this was probably the best advice I had ever had, "if your wife wants out of the marriage tell her to get out of the house". So I did, and I then found work, any job I could, to enable me to get a mortgage and pay her off. Never thought I would ever be a cleaner, but fellas, believe me it's not as easy as it sounds; I now admire and respect cleaners. It was a means to an end and I now enjoy my work. Life seems to go in phases and there are several phases in this book lol, and they have not held me back in MY LIFE AFTER MY WIFE.

PUTTING THE SMILE BACK ON MY FACE

Well here we go but please remember between all the fun I do have lapses of emotional turmoil and I do talk about them now and again.

I had a set amount of money in savings and decided that I was going spend some of it. Women call it retail therapy and guess what, lads? Now I know why so many women are walking around the town with a smile on their faces because when you let go and spend, it's fucking great! All those stupid things that she used to frown upon are now yours; you know, the flip flops that have a bottle opener fitted to the sole, all the clothes she said didn't suit you, the Armani watch, and then there is the biggy present to yourself. Mine was a little motor home I now affectionately call the "FUCK TRUCK". I'm Guessing that word has brought a smile to your faces and got you paying attention.

I don't consider myself as good looking by any stretch of the imagination, but both my exes were very attractive so I had something going for me and no it was not the size of my cock, because that's nothing to shout about either but I never have any complaints.

So now I have all the clothes, the jewellery (well a watch lol) and believe me as time went on and I started to gain confidence I also started to build a wardrobe of clothes that most men look at you in and you know damn well they are thinking he looks good. lol Actually some think you look a bit gay or who the fuck does he think he is? Guess what; it doesn't matter because you feel great and you look great.

Driving home after picking up the Fuck truck from the converters I had a call, and it was not a biblical one or a road rage driver stuck behind me in the middle lane; it was the mobile. I answered it, of course, on my hands free!!! It was an escort agency thanking me for the pictures and my part profile; "sorry," I said "you must have the wrong number and I am driving at the mo," so I hung up.

You know what it's like when you get a new toy. I am driving down the motorway at 60 mph because I am dead chuffed and spending more time looking around the truck than I was driving it. Of course everyone on the road that day was looking at it and thinking *wow great truck lucky bastard,* Well they were in my mind lol then I hit a traffic jam that looked like it went on for miles. Was I bothered? Was I fuck; it meant that everyone could see it better so I rolled down the window, arm out in the sun, looking dead pleased with myself.

The following Monday this agency calls me back saying about how I sent the pictures and put my profile online.

"Not me mate," I said.

"Yeah. Take a look yourself; here's the address."

So I took a look and there I was, So now I am thinking who has set me up? To cut a long story short he wanted to know if I was interested in work and if so to complete my profile. I wasn't sure about the whole thing at first so he gave me a day to think about it. Next day another call came, this time from a woman who ran through what would be expected of me. I was now feeling fairly confident that I could pull off a meeting so I agreed to a job for the following Wednesday, I had been briefed about location, client name, and what to wear; we also talked at great length about the initial meeting and the rules, so now knowing all this I decided to get some back-up. No not a minder or a reserve lol, but some pills (well for all I knew she may be a minger!! Lol) and of course some condoms, And getting them was funny. I am in town on the day before the meet in a well known cheap drugstore and I asked a male assistant where about in the store could I find the condoms. He walked towards a cabinet and pointed out a massive collection and said take your pick, mate. Well hitting on the mate bit I picked up a box of ten (you know, thinking I could be busy!!) and walked towards the till. Now people who know me will tell you I am highly coloured (red faced) at the best of times lol so walking towards a till with a box of condoms where a stunning seventeen year old girl is sat was not going to help, but I got fairly close to the till and because the floors had been wet there were strategically placed rubber mats on the floor to avoid people slipping, I get close to the till and then I tripped on the corner of a mat, the box fell out of my hands and rolled along the belt towards her at the till she quickly reaches out and saves them from going past like a pro goalkeeper, then looks at them, and then me. I quickly regained my balance and said "sorry, don't normally throw condoms at young girls", my face now looked as if I had spent all day in the sun, red and hot I must of looked a right twat, but I felt ok, not embarrassed about buying them just the way I tripped and threw them.

She smiled and said "£5.50 please, sir."

Well I nearly wet myself with her straight face almost disgusted that someone of my age would even be thinking of having sex let alone safe sex lol.

The big night comes around very quickly and I am suited up and looking good. I get to the hotel where we are going to meet about ten minutes early and the routine was to contact the agency to let them know I am in the foyer and then they contact the client and inform her. She turns up slightly late but, after all, she was paying so that's okay lol. I was surprised since she was not bad looking; a tad overweight but defo worth a squirt so now I felt quite good. We meet, she introduces herself then we sit and chat and she hands me an envelope. I remember all I have been told and take my leave of her a few minutes later and go to the toilets to count the money in the envelope. £500. Heart racing, red faced and temperature raised I look into mirror and see how red I am, There are several things going through my mind; cool down, breathe, stop looking like I am on fire, five hundred quid means four hours, starting to panic again now cus will it be four hours in a bedroom or will I get a meal a few drinks and a long chat hopefully for 3 hours and 57 minutes lol I finally regain my control and head back out; not giving her the envelope back means I have accepted the money and will carry out the deed lol.

Well things just got better and better as the time went by and we had quite a lot to drink at the bar and she was paying which is strange but I remember thinking I could get used to this. We eventually went up to her room with about an hour or so to go and luckily by this time we had got around to sexual likes and dislikes which is a turn on in itself when you're sat at a table in a bar talking in public about past sexual experiences and what she liked or didn't like. She said that I was very confident and that she had not met anyone as upfront and as open about sex as I was.

On my way to the room I thought about the situation I was going to be in within the next three minutes, I said to myself *don't pause get straight in there when the door shuts and get stuck in.* well the door did shut and I am inside this hotel room with a stunning women(remember I had drunk at least four stellas and a couple glasses of white) so I walk up to her from behind putting both hands on her waist. I look over her shoulder and raise one hand to move her hair back away from her neck, she tilts her head as I start to kiss her neck gently whilst putting both hands firmly back on her waist I raise my hands gently up her sides and down over her front, slowing down as my hands slide over her quite ample and firm bust. She relaxes and slumps back a little and I can feel the softness of her bottom relax into my now very hard cock; even through your clothes it is sexy. I run my hands back over her bust and slowly undo her blouse buttons and, not stopping to fully expose her bra and boobs, I move my hands back down to her waist and pull her toward, me ensuring she could feel the excitement in my trousers. I then slid one hand down the outside front of her trousers. She was dressed in a business suit but had removed the jacket earlier in the evening, I caressed her crutch area gently and then firmly ran my hands now all over her for as far as I could reach down while running my fingers through her hair, gently tugging at it as I moved down her head and onto her shoulders and boobs. I pulled her blouse out from her trousers and continued to undo her buttons whilst she is relaxed and I am still standing behind her, which makes the undoing of buttons that much easier.

I finally removed all her top clothing whilst caressing her body sensually. Her boobs were firm for their size and her nipples very hard and I noticed her get excited when I pulled on them so made sure I went back there every so often during undoing her trousers. They dropped down easily when undone and then she was stood there with her legs just a little apart in a very nice white thong which matched her bra; I like matching underwear. Her soft bottom was now firmly pushed against my crotch area and as I slid my hand down the front of her thong she pulled away slightly and put her hands behind her to feel my cock.

She played around with the tip and my bell end between her finger and thumb through my trousers and it was at this point I turned her around and kissed her. She walked backwards towards the bed and we stopped for a brief moment whilst she got onto the bed which gave me the time to take a prepared condom out of my waistcoat pocket and put it on the side. I leant over the bed and kissed her whilst she undid my trousers then I pulled away gently and took my trousers and waistcoat off but only undid my shirt not removing it. I could see her glance at my cock in my boxers so I removed them whist she was still sitting up on the bed and when she saw me do this she removed her thong, revealing what I had been caressing earlier; a very neatly shaped but very full pussy.

I then put on the condom and climbed on to the bed, putting my hands under her knees at the back of her legs lifting them up and open. I get right up to her and push my cock into her very wet pussy. I purposely did this gently for a few strokes then I fucked her quite hard for a few strokes. She enjoyed this and I could tell that she wanted to be submissive and looked like she wanted me to use her. Putting her into the position I call the "book keeper" which involved turning her on her side, keeping her bottom leg straight and her top leg bent, holding the bent leg behind the knee and pushing it up towards her head Then I straddle her straight leg so there is one knee each side her and pussy is fully revealed and so is her anus. The reason I call it the bookkeeper is because from here you can get a double entry lol and that's exactly what I did, I held her firmly and with alternating power and speed I fucked her pussy for a while. She obviously liked it from her sounds and movements she then out of the blue, and a lot quicker than I had expected, had an orgasm.

Well that is a confidence boost in itself and believe me it was also a relief because it took the pressure off a bit considering she is paying and that you have delivered. And partly because for that amount of money I would want a lot more so being the type of man that I am I wanted to make sure she got what she had paid for. After slowly fucking her through her orgasm I pulled out of her pussy and used the juices from her orgasm to lubricate her anus wiping it all around using my cock like a brush lol (couldn't think of a better way to put it lol) I then pushed my cock into her tight bottom and she groaned for a while but obviously liked what was happening. I again alternated between hard and soft strokes, I put her bent leg down and put two fingers into her pussy but only about an inch in maybe 1 ½ inches just to the point where she, like every woman, is very sensitive. I rolled my fingers around in this area, gently moving in and out at the same time.

Consequently she had a massive orgasm and it was hard for me to keep my fingers in there. I eventually removed them and slid my cock out of her bottom, and needed to replace my condom so I went over to my coat to get another condom.

"Do you feel you need since it's much better without," she said.

I agreed but insisted because of the risk and said I was thinking about the safety of both of us She never replied but was happy to continue as I pulled at her to get her on all fours at the end of the bed. I again slid a couple of fingers up into her pussy, this time all the way, and then withdrew them before sliding them up the crack of her bottom and around her anal passage then up under to her clit forcing her full lips apart. After a few minutes she was starting to move with the motion of my hand so at this point I turned her back onto her back and went down on her, sucking at her clit and moving my tongue around her lips, clit and hole with her legs apart and in the air.

I stood up and again put my cock up her pussy and I fucked her really hard. She loved it and was moaning with every thrust. I pulled out and got her back on all fours and continued to fuck her very hard, putting one leg up on the bed one hand on the small of her back and also pulling her hair. I fucked her for what seemed like ages; it must have been a good ten minutes I kept changing pace and she came again and shortly after so did I. It was not long before I got dressed and left but not before asking if she had enjoyed herself.

"Definitely" She replied.

Walking down the corridor towards the lift I felt like a right fucking stud lol with a smile as wide as my shoulders and excited over what I had just pulled off on my first night as an escort; a well paid escort at that, and it was at that point I remembered it was the first shag I'd had since my wife left me. No more right hand or left hand, come to that lol I found myself thinking *let's hope there's a lot more of this.*

Well there was more actually; quite a few more and I will talk about them soon but it was all downhill from here on in; size wise that is lol They seemed to get bigger and bigger and while they were all very nice people and there's nothing at all wrong with big women they're just not my type but when you are getting paid it is well worth the effort It was then I realised that I was actually learning things about women and about myself

Things that would prove to be very useful to me in the future, Especially when talking to women and especially on a one to one basis. I was finding it very easy to deal with in my head and even after a few paid jobs I was starting to think about dating sites as I really did, and still do, want to find the next life partner. I say life partner cus I will never ever get married again. Why you may ask? Well because at the age of 55 I cannot afford to lose half of what I still have, again, so my next partner has to be able to stand on her own two feet just in case it does not work out. Believe me when I say there's a load more to tell about women I got paid to escort and women I met on dating sites. Oh just one more thing before you rush off and sign up as an escort; don't pay anybody that runs an escort agency up front. If they ask it's a con. Also the free dating sites are the best ones. "Why?" you ask. Well because most of the women that are paying to be on a site that charges are also on the sites that don't lol so why pay to see them? And also, from experience, I have slept with lots of women from the free sites and only two from sites that charge for membership.

Okay more fun lol, The second escort job is about 2 weeks later and the second job involves a bit of travelling so this is where the fuck truck comes in useful lol Also Id better mention at this point that the site advertises me as good at role play and guess what? I am! lol Never thought I could act but, fuck me, I deserve an Oscar for some of my performances. Sorry; got sidetracked there for a mo. Got so much going on that I need to write about that it's hard to keep on track. lol I even get excited telling people. lol Well where was I? Oh yeah, driving up the M5 and a new job in the fuck truck; oh and a bottle of white in the fridge and a couple of glasses on the next shelf chilling. lol

I get there early afternoon. She is a buxom blonde and well built all over. She would definitely not damage her face if she fell over although she was attractive as well for a big woman. There was something I noticed but never saw it till much later—wait for it, wait for it—I will tell all in good time. We met that evening about five-ish. We sat at the van for a while chatting and I got paid as usual then we went out for a meal. She drove a very flash motor and I was petrified in the passenger seat but we got there and back safely. She paid for the meal and drinks and I still can't get used to that. lol, She was all over me all night; so much so that people in the bar and restaurant noticed but hey, they never knew me; or her come to that, so what the heck. And that is something to remember when you're somewhere where nobody knows you so practice being who you want to be. It may sound strange but we all want to but don't because of confidence usually. Anyway, getting to the truck it's not long before we are stripping off and then again it hits me there is something wrong here but the moment passes as she pulls down the front of my boxers and puts my cock in her mouth and she was good; I would say second only to a woman I met off a dating site. Whilst she is happily playing with my cock I am taking off my shirt and prepping a condom. She was so good I felt very excited and grabbed her head in my hands, pulling her head all the way down my cock then I held her head still while I fucked her face. lol Sorry couldn't resist that remark but it is actually what we do lol We stopped for a very short time and continued to take the remaining clothes off and it was then I noticed she was smooth; not just her pussy but her legs, arms, belly and back. All of her like she had been waxed all over and she looked like she had been oiled too. It was strange to see but nice to touch.

I was fucking her in all sorts of positions and she was loving it but when I attempted to enter her bottom she said no and fellas, that is a big rule with all women; NO means NO so I pushed it into her pussy. Very smooth and actually quite tight and she is on all fours and getting it good and hard. My body slamming into her ample bottom sounded like I was slapping her, the jerks from me banging her nearly brought the whole thing to an end and how I managed to keep going I don't know because as I banged her, her hair fell off. It was a fucking syrup! I just knew there was something not quite and right now, bent over in front of me, is a well oiled hairless big woman. At one point I did think, and this is honest, *fuck me it's a seal!* lol How I did not laugh or lose my hard on I don't know.

I returned home and picked my son up from his mother's who was living a mile or so down the road. I did allsorts with my son and

I was heavily involved in all his activities and always have been and I believe this was contributory to my wife falling out of love with me. You see, I think she became alienated from my son and I, let's face it, I took him to football on a Monday night, swimming on a Tuesday night, football again on a Wednesday and Friday night, a full game on a Saturday morning and then racing every Sunday for the whole day. I can honestly say it was rare to have a day at home over the weekend. At the same time she had only ever seen my son play a few times in a couple of years and she had only seen him race twice in four years but she did almost half the swimming lessons so she never really bothered either. I worked my socks off in the house we had, changing kitchens and bathrooms, putting extensions up and out, knocking down garages, building fences and landscaping the garden several times. Not just in our house but in my outlaws place as well. I am a committed person and I put everything into what I do. I love to help people out as much as possible to the point where I get stressed through not having my own space and yes, I really was my own worst enemy. I have learnt from it big time, believe me, but guess what? I still make mistakes and bad one's, I still open my gob before I engage the brain. I never really intentionally want to hurt someone's feelings because I hate feeling bad myself so I know what it is like but I do it especially when I am stressed and it is funny I get stressed easier if I am hungry. I have found that out myself over the last few years; sometimes I am aware that I sound like a know-it-all, and I hate people like that but I really have done so much. I have experienced many, many things in my life.

My son is with me for three days a week one week and four the other as he splits his time between his mother and me because we live either side of the school he goes to. I tend to have my darkest moments when he leaves to stay at his mum's and I can honestly say that I have come home and sat in a chair in my lounge for about four hours until it is dark, not realising where the time is going. No telly, no noise anywhere; just my thoughts of the past and how I let it all go. Sitting there with tears running down my cheeks, eyes sore from the salt in the tears, guts turning over and feeling dead depressed and I can really understand how some people can take their lives. I really have been low and I still get low at times but not that low anymore. I would say I have never thought about taking my life but have thought about people who have and feel like I can understand their loss. I am strong minded and a very positive person so I snap out of it very quickly.

I get another job, this time it's quite near Bristol. I have pills and condoms prepped and all my clothes travel up in the fuck truck but it's a hotel so it won't be needed. Shame; I like it in the truck. lol

Anyway normal form but I get to meet her in her room straight away and I am thinking *oh God, hope she is fit and hope she is not expecting four hours of sex.* I can honestly say I am nervous again. I get to the room and knock on the door and she must have been waiting with her hand on the handle cus no sooner had I started to knock on the door than it opens, which makes me jump a bit. Then I see her; well, I couldn't fucking miss her since she filled the doorway and I don't know if she could tell but I was trying hard not to be shocked and I was doing my best to smile and not run out the door. She was fucking ugly but that was not the worst of it; she was about a size 20 or more and the only safe place to fuck her would be a swimming pool where she would be a little lighter. lol I am seriously thinking about going and she turns and says "Wow, you're nice and you look fit. Do you think you can handle all of me?" and then she giggled she was confident but then most women who book an escort are.

"I'll just finish getting ready and we'll grab a bite to eat" she said.

"yeah," I said "that will be good, anywhere special in mind?".

"here at the hotel" she replies, "they have a great restaurant, and serve big portions."

Then she giggled again; at least she was aware of her size and that she ate a lot. lol And fuck me could she eat lots in short spurts! I thought I was gonnna spend the whole time watching her eat. lol Lucky we weren't at an all you can eat place cus they would be bankrupt from the way she was vacuuming it in. She must have had a mixer for a stomach because she hardly chewed her food, it seemed like it was just sucked in and swallowed lol.

Eventually we got to drinking in the bar and I got around to her sexual habits. She was very upfront with it and had definitely experienced many different sexual acts and she loved role play. So there was I wondering what she wanted from me. I couldn't see her being the submissive type and I hoped she is wasn't into wrestling. lol It turns out she wanted to be the naughty girl at school where the teacher makes her stay behind for being naughty in the class. Well as it happens she wants to be spanked, and anything more that might be associated with that scenario and sex and she wanted me to take the lead.

I was a bit nervous but confident so we went to her room. She said she wanted to go into the bathroom to get changed and she came out in a very believable school uniform for a girl/woman. BIG woman lol I turned off the main lights and put on a bedside lamp, and then started at her. I shouted not too loudly at her, saying that she was very rude in the class today and that's the reason she was here with me.

"You deserve to be disciplined," I told her. "I've had to use other methods in the past but they haven't worked because you're still being naughty so you leave me with no alternative, young lady!"

I then grabbed her firmly by the hand and pulled her towards a chair then I instructed her to bend over and told her that if she made any noise I would lift her skirt and spank her. I immediately slapped her bottom and she yelped a little; not because it was hard but because she wanted me to lift her skirt since it was all part of the role play. I then lifted her skirt to reveal a very big white bottom and a very small thong. Well I think it was small cus I could not see much of it lol I did actually spank her quite hard the next time and each smack was harder than the previous one. At the same time I told her not to make any noise as I would pull down her panties and really spank her. Of course she made the required noises lol so I went to pull down her thong and as I tugged at it they ripped and she seemed to like that and was very turned on by it.

I spanked her a couple more times then put my hands on the inside of her legs, gesturing for her to open them a little. With her standing straight legged and bent over the seat of the chair using it as a support I continued to spank her saying this is just the beginning, young lady, because today you are going to get punished properly. Her bottom bore the red marks of my hand and fingers. I slid one hand up the inside of her thigh up to her very wet pussy. She was natural and was very hairy down there which did not bother me at all. I rubbed her pussy and lips for a short period then again just putting my fingers in about an inch or so just to where it's very sensitive then rolling them around the ridge.

She was enjoying every minute of it so I knew things were going well. I then took my hand out from between her legs and started to spank her hard and she was now starting to move her bottom as I was smacking it so I told her to keep still or I would insert my cock into her bottom. She continued to move so, not holding back, I forced my cock up her bottom and fucked her very hard. She loved every minute of it, forcing her very large white ass towards me, almost pushing me over and definitely forcing me backwards. I consider myself a fit man with reasonable strength but I could not stop her reversing onto me. In the end I pulled at her hair like you would a wild horse and did my best to stand my ground. I don't know if you have tried this but to fuck someone this large is very exhausting and you use muscles that you have not used in a long time, especially at my age, but I managed to hold my own and showed her who was boss in this fuckathon.

Putting my hand on the small of her back I got enough grip to push her back towards the chair. I then gestured to her that she should move to the bed, without suggesting anything. She immediately laid on her back and raised her legs, more or less telling me this was the position she wanted to be fucked in now so I got on my knees and pushed my cock into her pussy for the first time. I start off with long, slow strokes; I say long I actually mean just as far as I could go. lol then

I started to pick up speed and banging it in harder and she is starting to moan. She is holding her own legs back which is a benefit as I don't think I could have done both, given the size of them. She is now very wet and not far from an orgasm so I keep pumping away faster and harder, driving the little fella all the way home every time. She orgasms but I don't ease up at all. I keep banging away at her full pussy and she comes down as I ease off so I with draw my cock and move her into the bookkeeper and I am back in again, pumping away with one hand on her hip holding her down and one behind the knee of her top leg. I have room to just keep pumping so there's no stress on me whatsoever as I am not supporting her at all.

She is loving this position and she puts her head back and brings her top teeth over her bottom lip moaning as I thrust my cock in and out fast then slow. I pump away at her pussy for some time, knowing that I may not be able to perform at my best if I was to fuck her doggy style so I just kept at it until she reached another orgasm and I certainly did my best to reach one myself. To be honest I wanted to get this over with but I did not want her to feel bad if I had not had an orgasm. She may not have felt good so I went for it and managed to fill the condom tip. lol I have been told that I have a large amount of cum and by more than one woman.

God I made it sound like I had a fire hose for a cock then, reality is the difference could probably measured in a teaspoon lol it just seems a lot to some woman, Well it would if you weren't getting any.

& Learning about Women and Things I/We Should Know

It was at this stage that a woman's body and mind were becoming something that I needed to know more about. The body bit was easy as anything you need to know can be found on the internet. I used the knowledgeable butler because he knows everything. And believe me you can put anything in; for example big labia lips, where the answers range from what men are asking and saying to what women are asking and saying, there was a forum and descriptions from medical experts. Put in vagina or pussy, and you come up with detailed information that you can use when talking and during sex. Women love it when they see that you understand their bodies and how they work; mostly they like it that you actually pay attention to giving them pleasure and not being selfish. Some men have the three minute syndrome; in, cum, out, sleep. lol NOT good fella's; not good at all! Oh and ladies? It's not all our fault since there are some of you who are selfish as well.

I also got information on the net about woman, sexual tips, vagina sizes, sensitive points on their bodies, how some women can have an orgasm through penetration alone and some who can from playing with their clitoris. The lucky ones are those able to have orgasms in many ways. Then there is information about women who are so wet with the thought of having sex, how the pussy throbs and the lips that swell and part; how sensitive the first inch to 2 inches are in a woman's pussy. So many things that I will say I knew but so many I didn't, including how some women prefer their boobs and nipples to be played with more than their pussies; how some actually love being fucked anally, even how some feel in command when giving a man a blow job. Spanking is a lot more common than you think and there are women that want to be spanked gently as it's the being spanked that is the turn on. It is naughty and that's great but there are some that want a really good spanking and that's great too as well, as long as you know when enough is enough. Remember you have to feel comfortable with what you are doing as much as she does or it won't work.

Talking about sex to a woman is embarrassing for some men and some women but the results of the conversation with the knowledge that you have learnt about what makes a women or your partner tick is very rewarding. Some women love being photographed; it is a naughty thing that only nude models do and oh my God! someone may see them so never, ever have the face in the frame; unless your partner wants that of course.

Sending a picture of your cock to a woman is not as big a turn on as them sending you a picture of their pussy. Why? Well it's that women don't necessarily respond to visual stimulation in the same way men do but woman are aroused by a tasty piece of erotic fiction !! and I have learnt this from talking to women; many women. lol Don't get me wrong; the sight of an erect cock does it big time for some women but a bulge in your boxers provokes a better reaction for most women. When I say talking to a women about sex is a turn on for both sexes in the conversation what I need to say here is that there are limits. There are things that are alright to say and some that aren't and those things can only be judged from the reaction you get whilst talking. I have found that being downright disgusting is a massive turn off but discussing different positions, scenarios and likes dislikes is the way forward. You would be surprised about how many women dream of certain scenarios from dubious consent to more than one man, spit roasting, bondage, blindfolded, men dressing up etc are just a few examples. There is also having their hands tied; some in front, some behind. Even some above or to the bed corners or posts. I have learnt that using handcuffs with padding so they don't rub and showing them how to release themselves if required is a must for most women That way they are more willing to try or take part.

Using toys (dildos) is great as well, especially for women as many of them can and want to have sex longer than most selfish men (sorry lads but it is true; we are selfish). Well I'm not lol but most of you are or so I m told.

I warm mine up in warm water and use a very good lube so it's more realistic. I also have ones with suckers on the bottom so you can stick a dildo to a wall or a floor and get the lucky lady to back on to it or sit on it and at the same time you put your cock in her mouth and there you have a spit roast but with only one man so the lady has her fantasy in safety and feels great about it. Obviously she may want the real thing next time lol but she may just be satisfied with her lot.

Lots more of that later; in the mean time let's move away from escorting and get to the dating sites.

🎵 Pay to date or
is **FREE** just as good?

I start off on a well known paying site. By that I mean you have to pay for membership. I am on there for about a month just looking and during the month I contact a few women and get the odd message from some that are not my type to look at so I reply out of politeness. I see one woman who comes from my city and send her a message but receive no reply. To cut a long story short I eventually get into contact on the Friday with just a quick message forwarding email address and we then swap emails for a day and agree to meet on the Sunday. She is coming around to mine and we will walk down to the local pub/eatery which is only a couple hundred yards away. She arrives in her Alpha Romeo car and she has blonde hair but as I was to find out later she is naturally brunette in colour, She is about 5'4" in her heels and quite slim and attractive so BONUS! lol She comes up to the door and knocks so I take a quick look into the mirror as a double check to confirm I am looking okay. lol I open the door with a smile and a cheerful "Hi!"

Well we eventually walk down to the pub chatting away; you know, the usual small talk lol And hey lads, don't make the mistake of talking too much and don't tell her your life story in ten minutes cus she will do a runner sooner or later. lol Don't talk over her either; let her finish even if she is boring and when she is talking to you maintain eye contact. Not permanently but often looking straight into her eyes and sit next to her not opposite. Be relaxed and open and this is really, really important; listen to her, mirror her body actions and relate to her stories. Don't have a blacker cat but inform her of similar things that have happened to you or a friend, be shocked and giggle at the right times . . .

Ooops, sorry where was I? Ah yes, down the pub with JUDY! That's her real name and she said I could use it. Well actually it's a shortened version of her real name "????????????" censored. lol Hi Judy! lol By the way Judy is helping me by reading this book at various stages so I hope she likes reading what I've written about her. lol We are actually very good friends and while we're not in a relationship with each other we do tell each other stuff; lots of stuff. It's great having a female as a best friend. We did have something at the beginning but it wasn't to be. lol

Anyway, I have been with her for about fifteen minutes and we are at the pub. I get us a drink and we sit in the bar chatting away, swapping stories and experiences and I tell her about being an escort. Why, you might ask? Well because I like to tell all and I don't like to hide things. Imagine her finding out three months later; not a good thing so I am totally up front. As you will find out some have made their excuse and left and others are intrigued and some want to know in detail. lol Well things are going great; we are laughing and getting on great but we get to the point when a decision has to be made. She has driven to mine and has had her allowance drink wise and I remind her of that. And because I am confident I also offer her to stay at mine if she wants another drink and I even offer the spare room—tongue in cheek, a little smile and a glint in my eye—and with a little persuasion she say yes to another drink and all that that entails. lol *The green light*

I remember thinking; *get in there* lol So we have a few more drinks; lol well, we are only walking now. lol I remember walking back hand in hand and laughing like a couple of school girls because we really did hit it off. Okay, okay I'm getting there!! We eventually get to bed—is that quick enough?—lol and the next bit may get censored cus she is the proof reader. lol

We are both naked and in my bed; well almost in it, and I am working my way down her body, kissing and licking as I go, pausing for a while on her nipples she was well into them being sucked and flicked with my tongue and nibbled with my teeth but she stopped me going any further.

"Why? I asked.

"I'm too wet to let you go down on me," was the answer or words to that effect. lol

And believe me she was effin soaking and right up for it. Needless to say I went for it and played with her pussy with my hand and fucked her in many positions until eventually she is sat on my cock, riding away and she says "God! I can do this every month, even if you just wanna be friends!"

I take her from behind and fuck her for what seemed like a very long time and she seemed to have at least five orgasms during this session. And for the record she had fair sized boobs with nice big sticking—out nipples and a very wet, close-cut, shaped pussy with nice lips soft to the touch.

We had several dates and she stayed at mine sometimes and I also stayed at hers. We soon discussed likes and dislikes and she liked her small little ass being spanked by hand as well as by slipper and she enjoyed walking into my house and immediately being taken out to the secluded back garden, bent over one of my wooden tables and taken from behind. She was so turned on by the thought of it happening that on her way here she would get wet in anticipation. I could feel this excitement as soon as I pulled down her panties and felt her pussy. I used to vary my strokes from slow and long to short and fast and one question she had for me was how come it takes me so long to come? Well I always thought women liked it rather than the three minute wonder they always complain about, Judy's reply made me think.

She said "Well when you come quickly, when having a so called quickie, it shows that you are turned on by me and come quickly with the excitement"

"I have done," I replied. "But not so much these days."

Which is very true. I have found that if I am mega turned on and I manage to get a shag then I will come very quickly. Another thing I have found is that I can come quickly and then carry on after a short break of playing with my partner with my hands or dildos then get another erection and get back at it, though it takes a long time to come second time around which has its benefits as most women will tell you. lol

Judy was the first of, shall we say, many from the dating sites. She was also the first to try the spit roast using a dildo. lol I also found out in discussion with her later that when I had gone to work the morning after using the dildo on her she was left alone at my house and used it again. She said it was a great toy so I have since bought her one of her own Judy and I have been friends for about 18 months we tell each other about our experiences probably not all of them in massive detail, but I have mostly got some great advice from Judy, not about sex but about mortgages and day to day stuff. She has been truly a great friend and hopefully will continue to be and to answer your thoughts NO we are not still having sex. We have done in the past when we have both been out of a relationship. If we go out for a drink and she has stayed over at mine she has slept in the spare room. We truly understand each other but she is not the person I want as a life partner and she knows that.

Thinking about how helpful Judy has been, after discussions about paying off my ex and getting a mortgage so I could stay in my house which I used to think I couldn't afford I would have to sell and buy something much smaller in a not so good area, but after talking to Judy she put things into perspective saying, everything was relative. If the price of your house goes up or down then so do the ones you would look at to buy so why not get an interest only mortgage over ten years so you can afford the house? By then my ten year old son would be old enough to think about leaving or be off to university and I would have had some great years living in a nice place then after about eight years put it on the market sell it and pay off your mortgage then with the remaining money buy an apartment or smaller house outright like you were planning to do anyway.

Well that was such a great idea; my interest only mortgage is easily affordable and I have, and will always have, enough equity in the property to buy another place when the time is right. She has done all sorts for me offering not just advice on money and the house but also on women and sex. lol So on my way through this LIFE AFTER THE WIFE I have met some great people and there's more to come; lots more really nice people and some effing awful ones, lol one of which I made a big mistake on but I will get to that in time.

I met lots of women on dating sites and chatted to loads more and I can tell you this; there are women out there that live there life like some of the X factor contestants. They think they can sing and some of the women I have met think they are average or slim, and some say that they are forty nine but are actually fifty nine some use pictures that are ten years old and some have their pictures adjusted to make them look slimmer. But worst of all is that some actually turn up on the date knowing that they have lied. The fucking cheek of them; the absolutely bare-faced fucking cheek of them.

I had been chatting to a Thai woman who lived about five miles away. Her picture was of a slim, pretty oriental lady about forty ish with long black hair. We messaged each other for a couple of weeks and she even had doubts about meeting me saying she was not sure if she liked me or not. Well I thought at the time she was nice so it would be worthwhile to push my luck and see how it went

Well we arranged a meet at a pub in the town centre so I'm wait in the doorway and she is late. I fucking hate people who can just turn up late as if it's their right because it shows they don't give a toss about you waiting and obviously think they are better so you must wait. Stop! Stop! Dave get off the soap box! lol Well she turns up in a car that looked like it was pushed there and she gets out and walks towards me.

My chin hits the floor in shock. She is about four foot ten in heels, and she is about four foot ten around as well. She walked with a severe limp and she was about sixty not forty and she had a fat drag ass. I was fucking speechless. I think I was in shock; there was no way I was being seen in public with this lying, fat, ugly pensioner.

She said "hi" but she said it in such a way it was like I was privileged to meet her. She defo had one of those mirrors at home that you see at the fairgrounds and she really did think she was special when really she was a moose; a fucking Daddy Moose!!! She then walked into the bar and I followed her in, still in shock, and she looks for an empty table and makes her way over to it. I look around and people are looking at her. Worse still they also look at me as if we are together so I slow down and feel myself colouring up because I am embarrassed by this and stressed and annoyed, almost like I had been robbed. She sat down near a group of people and they are all looking at me; at least that's what it felt like, so I get to the table and tell her exactly what is in my mind

"You should be done for misrepresentation. You have lied about your age, your weight, your more than obvious disability and what's worse you have wasted my time and money. I am not staying to buy you a drink so goodnight." then I look up and see everyone around looking us at me and her and I then know I am red in the face lol so I turn toward the door and walk out.

Let me just say I have no issues with disabled people at all but you should mention it when chatting on dating sites. Also I bet there are just as many men doing exactly what that woman did.

I am writing these stories of my past, my recent past at that, and I can tell you honestly not a day goes by without a tear in my eye. That was not meant to sound like a poem or a lyric in a love song, but just lately things have got real bad with money and work, but that's later. I can't tell it now because there's loads to come before this day but what I will say is I talk to people about some of my issues as a sort of release, to take a weight off of my mind. They say a problem shared is a problem halved and I do feel that but sometimes I feel like I should just keep it all to myself. I get the feeling people are looking down at me or they think I am weak but far from it; I am a strong person but I am in touch with my emotions now whereas I was not five or six years ago and the end of my marriage has made me even more emotional. Am I over it? Well I would say yes but it is just the constant battle with work and money etcetera.

I have made a date from the free dating site and she sounds nice from reading her profile. There is no picture online so I ask her for one and she sends me one of her in a bikini!!! *come on then get in there* I am thinking. Fit as fuck; bit old looking but still got it and fit body. So we chat for a while and find out we have a few things in common; for example we both need air to breathe, we both drive, we both eat food and we both drink lager. What more do you want for a perfect match? lol So we get off to a flying start and I arrange a meet; 7:30 in a very popular place. I am early as usual. The deadline passes and I have never been stood up before so I'm now just a fraction anxious. Five minutes pass so I send her a text to say I am here and waiting; not nasty or abrupt or anything but enough to let her know *get your butt in gear or I am outa here.* lol

She texted back saying *I am on my way over **the** walkway,* (which was about two hundred yards as the crow flies). Then she says *I am wearing red!!!!*

What's that then a fucking warning? I think to myself so I look over to the walkway and I see this blonde walking over the pathway. As I walk toward her and her toward me she seems to get bigger so I put my fingers to my eyes to make sure my contacts are sat correctly on the eye and it takes a few seconds for complete clarity of vision and by now she is fairly close. "OH MY FUCKING GOD!" She has a red dress, silky looking, very fitted, long flowing blonde hair, stiletto heels and I am FUCKING gob smacked. What a lying fucking cow. when I say 'fitted dress' I mean fitted around all of her spare tyres. No way spare tyres is being kind, these were full on wide wheels, the sort you find on the rear of an F1 car. Her hair was so dry and frizzy that you could see it sucking the moisture out of the air. Her heels were ORANGE and SPANGLY and oh my God! She had no idea at all because she really thought she looked good. She was about sixty years old, she was pig ugly, she had a full set of false teeth since I could see the join as she opened her mouth.

"Hi," she said.

I was silent again. I had been conned by an old biddy but I started to walk with her along the front and she found it hard to walk properly on the cobles I still had not said a word. People were looking at her and it was not in my imagination; they really were. Not just a few people but everyone because she was dressed as if she was on her way to a summer ball but looked like an old soak. I was very embarrassed and had to say to her "Sorry, my love; you're not quite what I expected so rather than waste any of our time I will walk back with you to where we met but then I am going, okay?" I thought it best to say it up front even though I wanted to deck the fat lying cow but I held on to my thoughts and was as polite as I could be.

Dating sites; what a minefield. You look at profiles of some really nice, attractive women and message them. You may get one answer, you may not get any and at times you think you must be ugly or have two heads. But both my exes are attractive and some women I have been out with are very attractive too; very pretty with nice fit bodies so what is wrong? I get messages from really old women, or women who are defo not my type. Without sounding as if I am bigheaded or anything like that, I think *"Don't they look at my pictures and read my profile? Can't they see that I would not be their type?" Even when I set out a check list/shopping list?* lol Well, sort of criteria; you know the kind of thing. I actually said at one point the height range, the weight range, the age range, dress size, how they must be the type to look after themselves, be able to support themselves and much more. lol But even then I got women who where the complete opposite still asking "I read your profile and like what you had to say, if you feel like meeting for a coffee please contact me." I would like to reply what part of my profile said I want an overweight pensioner who thinks that Gym is a popular menswear shop? Where did it say cosy nights in swapping knitting patterns? Fucking hell, ladies! I changed my profile four times with a soap box one, a rude one, and two which I thought would be great. Lol

Lots of women also look at your profile and hope that by looking at you, you will contact them so they won't actually make the first move.

Don't get me wrong; there are some genuine women on the sites and there are some that have modern thinking. Some have got to grips with equality but I must say some want all the benefits of equality and still think men should pay for everything and hold the door open and let them out of junctions as if they have priority cus they are female. lol

Actually I do treat women like they should be treated. lol I am a real gent and I will let them in the door while holding it open for them; pull out the chair and let them have my seat. but I only let women out of junctions because I don't want them behind me texting and applying makeup whilst they use their car like a dodgem. lol, At this point some women will think *what a twat?* But the real women who can read between the lines and can actually understand where I am coming from will be laughing with me.

So how do you win on the dating sites? How do you get dates? Well firstly you need to make up your mind what you want from them. Is it a long term relationship? Just a night out and sex? Or just to make friends with people for a chat now and then? Because what you want requires different approaches, and what you want has a lot to do with how you deal with things in your mind, What sort of person are you HONESTLY? Because you must be honest with yourself about who you are and what you want.

Me? Well I wanted the end result to be a life partner, but had made up my mind that I would continue to meet women until I found that special person, which included dating people that were not defo my type but could surprise me when we met. So I broadened my search criteria from my type to fuckable. Now that can be a very wide outlook to some people and very narrow to others. With me, well, it would be fairly narrow cus I am a fussy fucker. (Dual meaning)

You look through the profiles of the women on the site, and ladies, take note of this; a very, very high percentage of them put *love or like walking on the beach or the moors; it's a shame to waste our lovely surroundings; I am so looking forward to sharing the experience with a man rather than walking alone;* or words to that effect. BULLSHIT! When I walk along the beach and on the moors you're not fucking there, you lying cows. Lol *How can I be so sure they're lying?* you are thinking. *God, that's a bold statement.* Well you're right, it is, but I have met **thirty four** women and only 2 of them actually did what it said on the tin. Some of the women I met had never even heard of some of the local small coves and walks so that's how I can call them liars

So ladies be honest, please. And gents don't believe it until you see it.

I have met women on a date and they have not offered to buy a single drink; they have happily let me buy drinks all night and some have even had the balls to say shall we eat and order top of the menu food and then sit there, merry on the drinks and full on the food that I have paid for and not even offered to pay even half the bill. I sit there smiling but thinking *fucking bitch, grabbing cow, thick-skinned snake, tight—ass tart.* I think we used to call women like this scrubbers when I was a kid.

My next move would be to get around to talking about how I own my own house and have a motor home. All this is on purpose because these women are the obvious, easy-to-read grabbers of society. They are selfish females who think men are an easy touch, so I lead them further in telling them how much I have but not in a way that sounds big headed. And I also arrange another night out, preferably the next night and I offer to pick them up so that they can drink and I always choose an eatery close to my house.

So to cut a long story short I ask them back to mine and to me the second night is a challenge, a game. Can I get her into bed? There is no way I would have a relationship with this type of woman so why not go for the sex? Oh, by the way ladies, I know that some of you are smart enough and just use men like me for a night out and also for the sex. The people who know what they want go out and get it, and I admire women who are like that but I prefer the ones that go Dutch on the bill and want sex but not a relationship, like fuck buddies and I have had a few of them. The thing is to play the field whilst you search so why not have fun? Women want to play around as much as men but they are not as obvious as we are or as open as I am. lol But they are out there, thank God.

I must say that I have dated some really nice women that are pretty, aged between thirty eight and fifty six, from five foot to five foot ten, with nice figures who are nice people, genuine. Some of these remain friends to this day and all have paid their way. All of them also offered me help in many ways, but with each and almost everyone, I could tell that there was not going to be a long term relationship other than friendship, And even though sex was still on the cards, there was one that I should have tried harder with but I really don't think I was in the right frame of mind when we met. That is history but we are still very good friends and we, like all the rest of my female friends, like and accept each other for what we are.

More on dating sites and the tactics I use later. But for now more fun! I have to say at this point I have sort of forgotten in which order I met the women I am writing about. There were five women that I would say I really liked and I am led to believe they really liked me; well, that's what they said!!! And the others range from nice, entertaining, fuckable, outrageous, no chance and lying bitch. lol

So the lady I am going talk about now is a special woman; one who, like me, finds it very hard to be with a life partner and a woman who has had quite a few relationships, including up until many years ago, marriages. She is a very down to earth woman, comfortable in her own skin, and a go-getter. She gets what she wants, she is a survivor. She is well dressed, has a great sense of humour, great body and very she' pretty; a real head turner and great to be seen with. lol She has a good sense of rhythm and loves to let her hair down when out for the night. She has, like me, experienced many things in life with all the ups and downs. She has had good jobs, she has been well off and she has suffered loss and scrimped for a living so she is well in touch with life and all it brings. More than that though is that she has survived it all intact and is a very strong woman, but a softie at the same time.

WHY is he telling us all this for fuck's sake? I hear you say. Why? Well because I don't want you to get the wrong impression about this lady when I tell you what we got up to. For some people it may seem strange but to others perfectly normal and some wish they could do what we did/do.

I have just gone through the book and realised at this point I need to say that Toni along with a few others turned out to be great friends, these ladies will always have a special place in my heart and memory. I have massive respect for them, and that the lady who I had met and did not try hard enough with is yet to be mentioned in the book.

Well after the big build up you're going expect something special, and special it is. At this point I really want to reiterate that everything that has happened thus far and everything that you're going to read is very true; not made up, not fantasy, true. So let me go back to the beginning and tell you how it all started with this lady, it was yet another dating site that I was looking around and unusually I noticed a profile with no picture. I say unusually because I do not normally entertain profiles with no picture. Daft as it may seem I was attracted by the name as it was the name of my son's best mate who happens to be Toni's nephew. Don't ask why but I felt drawn to this person so I sent her a message.

Eventually I received a reply after she checked me out by looking at my profile and we swapped messages then email addresses and eventually I get the first of about five pictures.

Wow! Get in there my son! She'd 'ave it! Stunning was my first impression, but I played it cool and thanked her for the pictures. We arranged to meet in a pub on the front on a warm September evening and she had set out guidelines that I was not to attempt to kiss her or touch her. She did not want to be pawed at during the date, she preferred to get to know someone first before she allowed them to kiss her or even hold her hand.

I need to say now I am a good dresser and I'm fussy about my clothes. My jeans are in shade order in my wardrobe and my shirts are in colour order as well. Actually all my clothes are in order. I have trainers to match all my tops and I even wear matching socks and pants. Extreme, I know, but that's me. Oh and I should say that my socks always blend in with my trousers / jeans and trainers. I will always wear matching clothes every time I go out; except for work where I put anything on as long as it looks half decent. lol I have paid up to two hundred quid for a jumper and well over a hundred for most of my good jeans. That's maybe not much to some people but mega for the average person. So what am I trying to say? Well I am saying that when I go out I look good, feel good, and above all I am very confident. So yes, I was nervous as she was a stunner; but hey, I am no Shreck!

I am waiting outside the pub for a short while when she walks down the drive. I smile, of course, but inside I am thinking *FIT*! But hey, not giving anything away I wipe the dribble from my chin, say hi and gesture for her to walk ahead as I open the door to let her enter. As I do this I get a moment to check out her butt and yep, it's all in the right place. Once inside I ask her what she would like to drink, so she asks for a coffee. I feel myself fall backwards but not actually move. *COFFEE* eh? But not wanting to make it look like I am a moron I order a Stella. lol I ask her where she would like to sit, she points as she walks toward a settee. I follow and pull a chair out of the way and once she is seated I go back to the bar and collect the drinks. I return and sit next to her and compliment her for her clothes and she reveals she had worked in the fashion industry for quite some time in the past and she then was very complimentary about my choice of clothes for the first meeting.

As we talked two women and a man walked past the back of her chair. I looked up.

"Pretty, weren't they?"

"Actually, yes they were," I replied and I laughed. I could tell straight away this lady demanded my full attention. She had probably been badly hurt in the past by some cheating lecherous perv. lol Okay, a bit strong lol but she had obviously been let down, probably several times so I spend the rest of the night firmly fixed on her face and when she looked around I checked her body out. We had another drink and the night was flying by. I was attracted to her and I could tell from her body language and how she smiled looking into my eyes that she was attracted to me.

Well, as time went by we met several times and one night early on in the relationship we planned to go out for a meal. Now I am dressed to kill lol and ready an hour before it was time to go when I realised I had not got any cash on me. I flew down to the cash machine and put my card in and pushed the required buttons and the fucking stupid machine kept my card. I started to sweat and felt myself getting anxious; after all, I am meeting a very sexy, hot woman for a romantic meal and I have no money. Thinking on my feet (well, I was stood up at the time!) lol I remembered I have another card another account but no money in it so I rush back home and log onto my account on the internet. I then transfer money from one account to the other but during this my account gets frozen. *What the fuck is happening?* I ring the company and tell them of my dilemma and who do I get on the other end? Yep, you guessed it; Bombay Bill who only knew these words . . . "Yes, sir, how can I be helping you?" "I will be doing my very best, sir."

So i'm thinking he will sort it in a mo then just a few seconds later he comes back with "Sorry, sir, I am afraid to say I cannot help you in this matter" so I hang up and then phone the lady who is just about to leave her house.

"Hi,****. Sorry but I have had a disaster. The cash point machine took my card," and I went on to tell her the whole story.

She laughs and says "That's okay; I will pay and you can pay next time."

Well not wanting to let her down I go to meet her and it was a great evening. We end up walking along the front, looking out at the sea, and where we have our first kiss in the back of (you guessed it!) the "FUCK TRUCK" which I strategically parked earlier that evening.

Day's passed weeks went by we are into the end of the third week and I finally get her at my house and on my bed where we had sex for the first time. I've got to admit here that I did not perform to my full potential as I was extremely excited about getting it on with her. Well to cut a long story short after about another week she decided I was not her type and she ended the relationship, But all is not lost since the lady comes back on the scene some time later and we have some great times, starting with texting, and then phoning each other. In our texting we start getting very open with each other about our likes and dislikes sexually and since she knew of my escort past and had actually been on the escort site and read my profile, which actually states that I am very good at role play, this is right up her street as she has always fantasised about certain scenarios but never tried them out. So it was an opportunity for her and great sex for us both was about to happen, cutting out the build up and getting straight to the first night of role play.

Picture the scene; I am a doctor and a friend of her make-believe husband. We have discussed her make-believe husband in our texts and now the texts we send each other differ in that we send normal texts as in us as our real selves but when it's the scenario build up she sends a text as the wife of my friend and will also send me a text as the husband so that the whole scenario has a true-ish build up, like painting the picture. Some might call that strange but it's not really since it's taking role play to the best level by getting as close to reality as possible.

So she has texted me and he has texted me (GET IT? I hope you do otherwise you're a lost cause!) lol He says *I want my wife fully examined mate as I am sure there is something wrong down there.* I say "Ok, mate, leave it to me," or words to that effect. It was much more involved than what I have just said but I am sure you get the idea. she texts and says her husband wants her checked out but she wants to know if her husband has done her any damage because he continually abuses her and fuck's her hard; not just with his cock but with other things as well and sometimes he holds her down while he lets a friend take her as well. So now the scene is set and she is due at mine for the first live role play. All the texting and phoning has been done, the story is set up and we both know what's going happen; well, up to a point anyway. I have a quilt on my kitchen table covered by a stretch sheet hooked over the four corners of the quilt and table. There's also a 'V' pillow at the top and paper towel at the foot end, the blinds are closed and there is a light on. The chairs are down one wall and on the worktop I have my lub and dildos set out like medical instruments and I must say I was impressed with my surgery. lol Oh, I almost forgot I also have a blindfold and plastic gloves that she loves the sound of when they are being put on, so I am all set up and just need the patient.

Remember this is role play and I think it's of a good standard since it's not just playing at it but carrying out a realistic act, I look out the front window and see her little sports job arrive and I watch her get out. She was dressed as she said she would be, like a business woman in a grey skirt suit with black stockings and high heels. Wow! She looked fucking stunning! She had a great body, as I have said, and she was very pretty as well so you can imagine the thoughts I'm having now when I see her walking toward my door.

GET IN THERE MY SON, YOU LUCKY BASTARD!!! FILL YOUR FUCKING BOOTS!!!

I open the door and invite her in with a welcome kiss as a friend and lead her into the surgery. I help her onto the bed telling her that I was going to give her a thorough examination and some of it may hurt a little.

"That's okay, doctor," she says.

I undo her blouse a little, just enough to reveal her breasts; well most of them and I then put my hands in and examine them. I suggest it would be better and make her feel more relaxed if she were to have her eyes covered as if in darkness, so I then slipped my blindfold over her head. once she was blindfolded sound would play a big part like putting on the medical gloves.

I felt her boobs again, this time bringing her nipples out of her bra and blouse. I then sucked and licked, biting on them enough to make her squeal a little and flicking her very erect nipples with my tongue. She was close to an orgasm and I had not got anywhere near her pussy yet. I undid my jeans and took them off then I put my hands on her head and turned it sideways. Standing slightly on my toes I put my cock at the entrance to her mouth and with one hand on her head and the other on my cock I pushed it into her mouth. She was surprised but sort of semi expecting it and I held her head whilst I pushed my cock in and out. She soon took over the movement and brought her hand up to hold my cock. She was really going for it as if the ice lolly was melting quickly on a hot day. lol

I withdrew and went to her legs, lifting from behind her knees and keeping her ankles together I lifted her legs until her thighs were almost 90degrees to her body then still keeping her ankles together I parted her knees, Revealing the tops of her stockings and her panties with the white flesh of her upper thigh standing out between the black stockings and her black panties. This was the time to put on the gloves so as she laid there blindfolded, legs open and leaving nothing hidden with her boobs on show and looking extremely sexy, she could hear the gloves being put on. I slid my hand down the inside of her right thigh and onto her pussy where I gently caressed her mound, moving her panties around beneath my hand and just managing to run my fingers over her full pussy lips. She had a very neat one inch line of well trimmed soft pubic hair beneath her panties. I slid my finger in one side, pulling the front of her panties to one side and revealed her very moist and very flush pussy, her lips just slightly open with the glisten from a very reddish-pink wet slit between them. She was visibly excited at me pulling her panties to one side, and then I used some lube just to make it easier; not that she needed any lube as she was well moist by this time. But she liked the feel of the lube and it never fails. I was sliding my fingers through her pubic hair and down over her mound and then back up, opening her lips and then running my fingers back down each side of her clit before opening her lips fully. Carrying on down and inserting my fingers up into her very wet pussy; she was easily entered with the tips of my four fingers and then coming out and up over her pussy again before pulling her juice up over her clit and lips then sliding my fingers back down, driving two of them all the way in; really high up into her. She loved this as she moaned and started to move with my fingers and it was not long before she had an orgasm.

I removed her panties completely and reached out for one of the vibrators that she had brought with her. Holding a small bullet-like vibrator on her clit and using a rather large vibrator to thrust away in and out of her pussy she orgasms again. She was now very wet and I was getting immensely horny playing with her and watching her gyrate on the vibrators. I led her off of the table, undid her blouse completely and played with her boobs whilst she was stood up next to the table still blindfolded.

I turned her around and bent her over the table, pushing her down on to it so all her weight was supported by the table, with her skirt lifted up over her little ass and her legs fairly straight and still in her heels, I take my cock out of my pants, grab hold of her hips and fuck her from behind very hard. She is moaning big time and loving every minute of it but just before I come I withdraw and get the large vibrator out again. She holds the little bullet-style vibrator on her clit herself and did so throughout the next twenty minutes whilst I fucked her hard with the vibrator. My arm and hand were aching and she was bucking away and moving all over the place while having several orgasms.

Eventually she squirts and it runs down her legs whilst she is having this orgasm. I get my cock out again and really bang away at her pussy then I change her position and lay her on her back on the make shift examination bed, moving her pussy and bottom close to the edge and holding her legs up. I can get all my cock right up into her and I can also bang her very hard from here and I did so for at least fifteen minutes. Now these times may not seem very long when you're talking about them but when you are laid on your back or bent over a table getting continually fucked it can seem a very long time and you use a lot of energy. So much so that she had to rest for a couple of hours on my bed before she was able to go home. It was very tiring for me as well but I loved every minute and looked forward to further consultations. OH YES there was more to come; lots more.

But in the meantime let me tell you about another incident when meeting a very nice lady from a dating site. I want to stress again that I'd never seen or dated more than one person at a time but I would admit to talking to other women on the dating sites but only to answer messages sent by them to me and even though I am going to talk about this next woman she did not come onto the scene until after the one that liked me as her doctor. lol So even though I mix the stories of the two up they were not taking place at the same time.

Well I arranged to meet in a bar in the city centre for a drink and a chat to see if there was any chemistry; to see, if we get on and have anything in common. She turns up and we are in the same bar where I met the Thai girl you know, the one with the limp. lol She is a very attractive blonde with a good figure; a size twelve but a firm, toned size twelve about five foot four inches tall with a nice butt and very ample boobs and a nice personality We talk for actually three hours so we definitely got on. lol We were attracted to each other and during conversation found we lived a few hundred yards apart, we had gone to the same school and we both knew a lot of the same people. Well we got onto talking about keeping fit and she brings up cycling

"I have a mountain bike that I like to ride" I say.

"Wow! Do you fancy a ride tomorrow" she asks,

"Yes, why not" I reply,

Now when I say I like to ride my bike I am talking about, you know, around the local reservoir for about four miles and stopping half way for a picnic. You know the sort of thing; making a Sunday afternoon of it.

So we leave the bar and I take her to her car which was a very nice little convertible in black. I kiss her goodbye and I make my way home, not giving the ride another thought. Morning comes around and I go to the garage and get out the bike. It's about a year or so old the tyres were not fully inflated. But hey, I am only going over to her house and then a ride up the local valley track!!!! So I give it a quick wipe remove any cobwebs. Yes cobwebs; there were actually some on the bike lol and I am dressed in jeans and a hoody cus it's not too warm.

I cycle over to hers; or at least I get to the top of her road and I am blowing out of my ass big time so I stop at the top to get my breath back. When I am feeling good I roll down her road looking for the house number. Well I didn't have to bother cus she is outside ready and waiting and oh fuck me; she is in full cycling attire and has a Trek lightweight mountain bike, wearing a definitely—done-this-before look. Well I didn't want to show that I was impressed by her outfit and I really didn't want to let her know I was intimidated by her obvious professional look for a short ride up the local track

"Yep, all ready to hit the road, you lead I will follow," I said.

And that was a good move, fellas; remember that it's best to follow a woman cus you can travel at their comfortable speed. Oh, and of course I get to check out her butt in Lycra. BONUS!

Well we get to the top of her hill; you know the one I rolled down and I am already sweating like a swamp donkey on a humid afternoon in the rain forest. She stops and asks if we should go over the top of the hill and up the valley or go down to the start. Well I knew the start was all downhill but it was also about a mile away and after only having done about three hundred yards up hill before I am blowing out my ass and the fact that I am a man I suggest we go up over the hill and down the other side to the valley"

She's okay with this so off she goes and I am doing my best to stay right up her tight lycra-d butt, But she is relaxed on her saddle and pulling away from me easily up this mountainous hill. okay it was steep but *seemed* mountainous. It also seemed to go on forever, at least five hundred yards. Hey, that's a long way when it's up the side of a mountain! Well we are only just into the start of the ride and she has stopped at the top of the hill and saying something that I couldn't hear because I was still coming up the hill and a long way behind her. I eventually get to her and cotton on to the conversation; it was about the view,

"Oh yes," I said. "Lovely," when fuck me I was roasting hot, out of breath and could not see a damn thing cus my eyes were blurry. There was only one decent sight and no, fellas 'twas not her butt, but the fact that from here it was downhill whichever way we went.

So off we rode; well rolled, actually, down a very long and steep hill. Oh yes, I was in the front leading the way and my God the cold air was a blessing. We got to the bottom of the hill and started on the track up the valley. Now, Not having done this route before I had no idea that it was slightly uphill all the way. It was not long before my legs were starting to feel it; a burn in the thigh muscle that I just knew was gonna make me suffer in the very near future. She is well ahead and by now realised that I was not quite the cyclist she was, so being a very thoughtful lady she stopped every so often and took in the sights that were on offer.

For me this was great because I had chance to get my breath back and rest my muscles and apart from the stunning view of the woods and rolling hillsides there was the bonus of watching her butt, especially on the rare occasion when she got out of the saddle and bent forward toward her handlebars. lol We stopped at regular intervals and I could feel myself getting a second wind. lol She was, of course, not even breaking into a sweat and every time we stopped she asked me if I felt okay to carry on further and of course not wanting to seem like a lightweight and of course the old male pride raised it's stupid head.

"Yes, let's keep going." I said." Unless you have had enough. I don't mind if you wanna turn back now." I was secretly wishing she would suggest we head back, but oh no, she wanted to carry on. Well there was this tunnel coming up; I had heard about it from many people and it was now about five miles into the ride. We emerged from the tunnel back into daylight and stopped just after and I was thinking to myself it had been a short section this time, not realising that we had stopped so she could brief me about the hill.

"Just around the corner is the bottom of a very steep hill," she said. "I always go up slowly, just sitting on my saddle, in a low gear. There is a rest point that I use just before the top we'll stop there, okay?"

I nod and smile as if it's no problem and say "lead on." Well off we went and like she said just around the corner there was a steep hill; so steep that it was only a couple percent off of needing ropes for safety. I almost had a heart attack looking at it and my energy was sapped at the thought. And knowing that this is gonna hurt big time but not wanting to look like a I can't handle the pace, I go for it. Oh by the way she had asked several times on this voyage of discovery if I was okay and being a very stupid man with more pride than I need, I engage my mouth before my brain.

"Yes, I am fine. It's a great day so you keep going and I will follow."

What a twat! why didn't I just confess I was not used to this like she was and suggest we call it a day, and head back maybe we can do it again very soon? But no; I do the man thing and that's why I am at the bottom of what seems like Mount Everest and already in pain. By now she is a good ten yards ahead and moving away slowly, my heart is pounding and the sweat is pouring off of me, my temperature has got to be close to boiling point and my heart is about to red line. Apparently it does this just before it flat lines. lol I look up and she is sat on her saddle pedalling away like it was not an issue and that did it for me. I just could not manage to stay on so I dismounted and walked the rest of the way up and there she is waiting at the rest point having a little drink and breathing like nothing had happened whereas I was blowing out of my ass big time.

Well we admired the view and talked about the sheep lol and then she said "she suggested we leave and stop for a drink at the local" Phew! Thank Christ for that; a drink. I get back on and with the thought of the ride coming to an end and with a nice little drink to look forward to I found some lost energy, although my ass was getting a bit sore by now and my thighs are at burn-out so the watering hole sounded great.

We get to this village which I knew but had only ever driven to and the local was open so in we scurried Well I did; she sort of ambled in and she asked me what I would like to drink and at the same time saying she is having a glass of warm water. *WARM WATER ?* I cant help thinking, *Fuck me, she is some sort of fitness fanatic and health freak, dressed like a pro cyclist on a very nice bike and drinking warm water and obviously does this a lot!* So I start to talk to her about cycling only to find out that she rides everyday and has been on many a long bike ride. Compared to her I am dressed in jeans with one leg tucked in my sock and wearing a hoody. Well I thought I looked good when I left my house this morning.

So there we were for about half an hour and my legs were starting to stiffen up. She had finished her WARM WATER lol and I had drunk my pot of tea. YES, okay, A POT OF TEA. Well I had to sort of try to fit in, you know; go along with it a bit because I could hardly ask if I could have a Stella could I, Well we make our way out to the bikes and I was thinking how it was uphill all the way here so it must be downhill all the way back so easy life. But to my amazement we turn right and home is left. Not wanting to sound like I could not take any more I say "Oh where's this lead?"

"This goes to the local reservoir just a few miles up the road," she replies.

JUST A FEW MILES UP THE FUCKING ROAD?!!! That was my thighs shouting since my mouth was not capable of speech at this time. so she turns and heads off and by this time I was beginning to think she was doing this on purpose and for a nanosecond I believe I was capable of knocking her the fuck out but looking at her flowing blond hair and her licra-clad butt I soon came back to sanity and hoped that there may be a pot of gold at the end of this rainbow. So the voyage is restarted and we are pedalling along a road where the wing mirrors of cars are just inches away from my handlebars as they fly past. To make things worse we are now in quite a strong headwind and I now know the route we are taking and I know how far it is to go till we get to the reservoir and that knowledge is enough to sap your energy. lol

Well we eventually get to the reservoir and the last section is a downhill run so that was great but just as I was thinking *thank fuck we are here* she turns around.

"Which way around do you wanna go?" she asks

Well my heart sank cus I know it is four miles around the reservoir and then there is still the trip back. so I soldier on; lol well I was in the army when I was younger. lol To cut a long story short the trip back was very difficult. My thigh muscles were burning big time, my body was getting stiffer all the time and I was very quickly running out of energy, even though when we got as far back as the warm water stop lol I knew from there it was all downhill but it was still painful. We eventually got back to the bottom of my hill and she asked the number to my house, "I will meet you there" I said, Because I had now got off of my bike to walk up the hill as I could not pedal another yard.

"When we get back I will give your aching muscles a rub," she said.

Wow! methinks *This could well be worth it!* lol So when I get back she is waiting in the driveway so I put the bikes in the garage and invite her in. I made a drink for us both; I had tea lol and she had WARM

WATER lol but after about fifteen minutes or so she offered to massage my legs. Not wanting to turn this down and because my whole body was now aching I told her to go for it, so she suggested I lay on the floor and I didn't need to be told twice, She starts at the bottom with my feet and works her way up my leg to my thighs and then further up to just below my now semi erection; first one leg then the other. she tells me to turn over and I do, again working all the way up my legs and actually on to my butt.

"ooh firm" she comments.

"ooh sore" I respond.

I turn over for her to continue with my thighs and she said "oh my that looks interesting" looking at the bulge in my jeans I told her to feel free and within seconds she slides her hand up over it time and time again. I now seem to have lots of energy; it's funny how if you take enough blood from your tired muscles and put it into your cock how good your muscles feel, or is it just being a man? You know, fellas, led by our cocks but does it really matter?!!!! Because when you're up for it and it is there for the taking us men are sluts; well I am anyway. before long she is removing my jeans and boxers to reveal a very solid erection so she wastes no time in getting her mouth around it and my word, she is very good at it as well. The pain of the cycle ride has gone and the pleasure of the next ride is about to take over and it's not long before I suggest we go to my bedroom where it is a tad more comfortable. I start to remove the Lycra; sorry, I start to peel off the Lycra and reveal very full boobs with very neat nipples and work my way down her body as I pull down her bottoms. Her butt seems to want to get out and I want to get it out and it's not long before she is lying on my bed and I have her in the missionary position just slowly fucking her nicely trimmed pussy and here is another woman who is very fleshy in the pussy area which is one of my favourite things. I love a full pussy one, with big flush lips but also very neat and this lady has it all well groomed and shaped; full and neat lips and a very neat and tight entrance, She also has a very well tucked away little clit so almost perfect and I like to look at what I am doing when I am fucking so I get her into the deep stick position followed by the bookkeeper and then doggy style.

She confessed she liked the way I fucked and I loved the way she was willing to do anything position-wise. And she was not shy; she knew exactly what she wanted and she made sure she got it. More women need to take that outlook. Why pussyfoot around? We all need it and we all want it in different ways so get what you want when you can fulfil the fantasies and live out those scenarios. It is not embarrassing as we all want to do something that rocks our boats so don't get to a point where it's too late and you wish you had.

She went home but we met on a regular basis, especially to ride our bikes, and with every ride I get better and better; even on my bike. lol No seriously, I'd learned about the little things, like having the tyres fully inflated lol, and one day I take a turn on hers and realise the advantage she had with a good bike. I never thought that there would be that much difference. I should have realised it really as I do with clothes since I always buy good quality attire, There's nothing wrong with the cheap shops but if you want your item to stay in shape and feel as well as look good even after it been worn several times and after many years, then buy quality because it makes sense. so I went out and

I bought a half-decent bike as well as some semi slick tyres, OH MY GOD WHAT A DIFFERENCE! I was flying and could not wait to get her out on a ride.

Well I have been seeing **** for some time now; must be about three maybe four weeks lol Well that's a long time for me. She has become someone whom I see most days and chat to or text to everyday, She is what I would call a tree hugger. No, that's harsh, but she wants to save the best parts of the planet. Lol She rides her bike to work daily thus saving fuel and the ozone layer. lol I am not taking the piss but just trying to give you a picture of the lady. She is the creative type, into flowers and plants and very frugal with her money, dedicated to spending as little as she can but living as comfortably as she can. Not tight cus she would pay her way and would be the sort to help you out if you needed it. She dressed well; not all to my taste but, hey, she has her own mind that's great. if I was to pick fault I would say that she is a little overweight probably through diet rather than exercise cus she does loads of that, and actually I have eaten out and in with her and would say her diet is not too bad either so maybe there is another issue somewhere. Don't get me wrong because she is not fat at all. I just like well toned and size ten but then I am too fussy I should be grateful just to have a nice person that likes/loves me.

**** has many, many friends from all walks of life; from well-off business types to not-so-well-off shop floor workers. She cares for elderly people as part of her work and does many other things to earn a crust, and I must say she knows how to make a living since she owns her own house, had paid off her ex many years earlier and then worked at several jobs as well as bring up her daughter and pay off her mortgage.

So this is a mentally strong woman who knows what she wants in life and out of life. Maybe if we had met a few years down the line when I was more settled we may have had something special but when we met I was not and am still not sure what I really want in a woman. I am not sure if I will ever be able to have a woman live with me again, although I want women in my life as I get on well with them; better than I do with men. But I have been spoilt with having my own space so when I meet a new woman I want to see her but not every day. I also want to text her but again not every day. Maybe just a short message to say 'hi, good morning' or 'hi, how's your day been?' But not much more as there's always lots to talk about at the beginning of a relationship but many people want to tell all inside a week and that's not me. Don't get me wrong; I want to talk about me because I can be confusing and give out wrong signals. I am very confident and very friendly as well as touchy feely and I can come over as 'you're the one I want' but actually I am just being me and I treat everyone the same way. That is I treat everyone I like the same way and everyone I fancy the same way, but people I don't fancy I will say up front. My problem is I can have sex with anyone and have a great time and do my best to give them a great time but it does not mean that I want them or to be in a relationship with them. I can deal with it in my head easily and hate it that I may hurt someone's feelings if I had sex with them without the relationship; that's why I am so upfront with what I say to them, and that's why I can carry on doing what I am doing. I don't feel guilty because everyone I have had sex with knows the situation and the outcome and guess what? From the four or maybe five people I really got on with four of them are still very good friends. I went out with one last night and she came back to mine and yes we had great sex. She went home and picked me up the following morning to drop me off so I could pick up my truck. lol Then we parted and made tentative arrangements for a wedding she has been invited to in a month's time as she had asked me to go with her.

Now I know that may change; it will change if she meets someone she really likes or if I meet someone and we both accept that may happen and I will not feel rejection if she calls and tells me she has met someone and would like to take him to the wedding. That's how it is; first and foremost is the relationship you're in or getting into. I am 100% faithful when I am seeing someone and I never have sex with anyone other than the woman I am seeing. Oh and just in case anybody is wondering if I do see more than one woman at a time? lol Well to be absolutely honest NO! I can talk on the phone or text all my friends, the ladies that I am close to, but I will never cheat on the new lady or the old lady. lol So hope I have made that clear, and hope that you people reading this, men or women, have the same principles as I do. Oh and also, my four close friends, the women, all have relationships that they tell me about; they go on dates and they tell me, they text me and I know about what they get up to. I know that may sound bad but they can talk to me and ask me things and if I know the answer I offer my advice sometimes it is just a listening ear, I do have sex with them if they want to even when they are seeing someone, It is they're choice but as I have said I never have sex with any of them if I am seeing anyone.

Some of you may be thinking now wow! what a great life he and his female friends have, But, hey, a reality check here; this little group I am in we are all looking for Mr or Mrs right to walk into our lives and we are all open to the fact that it could happen at any time and I will be really happy if any of my great friends meets that life partner. And I hope I get an invite to the weddings. lol After all, you can't beat a great wedding 'do'.

Let's make things a little easier by giving them all names. The naming idea actually comes from a woman I dated who lives fairly close to me. We have never had sex but we have met and we do go for a drink every so often to catch up but she started to give names to my friends and herself so she could understand who I was talking about. lol

So let's start with Judy. Well I know she has her real name here in the book but when I talk about her I refer to her as Spain. This is because she owns a property in Spain, as well as the one in England. She is also one of life's workers, a genuine lady who knows what she wants and won't settle for anything less. We get on great, really great, and we understand each other and probably use each other. I know her family and her nephew is my son's best friend as I said before.

Next is Bike. Well that's the lady with the bike; lol the very keen cyclist. Now let's be upfront here; she is not a bike in the sexual meaning of the word bike it's just an affectionate name I have given her.

Then there is Role Play. lol I think it's obvious who this is, and for the dim ones reading that is the lady who likes to think I am a doctor. lol,

Also there is Cornwall. Now she is a very nice woman but she lives too far away and another who I could not have given the rest of my life to. She lives in the darkest depths of Cornwall whose mother, sister, and auntie are the same person. lol The way to tell a person from this part of the country is when they are not wearing shoes and socks look down and you will see webbed feet. Not being disrespectful to the Cornish because I am only joking and they are exactly the same as you and I. It's a local thing, banter between connecting counties, I am sure it happens between every county in the country.

Last but not least is the newest of my long term female friends. I have called her GOK. Why? you ask. Well for two reasons really. One is that she is a union person, not a shop steward, but that seems to fit you know; Gok and shop. And also because she likes my advice on what to wear and what suits her so I call her Gok,

Well if you're keeping up you will remember that last night I went to a birthday party and I went with role play. We had a great night dancing and drinking, both of us dressed over the top for the occasion but that's what we are like. We got a taxi back to mine and in the taxi she leant back on me whilst I pulled her skirt up on one side. She was sitting behind the driver so he could not see that I had pulled her pants to one side and was playing with her pussy, sliding my fingers in and out and when we got back to mine I had to help her in as she was a little squiffy lol I then helped her towards the kitchen where I had prepared the dining room table as an examination table again. lol Needless to say the same scenario unfolded as before and we played and fucked for the best part of an hour until eventually I got her a taxi home.

In the past role play like all of us go through what I like to refer to as sex fests. That's a time that we all go through; well I do. It's when I am up for sex all the time. Of course there is the down side because there are times when you don't want sex. I have them as well but I don't blame it on a headache, ladies. And lads, I don't pretend to be asleep or even very tired and I actually tell the truth; I DONT WANT IT! lol

So a while had passed since the last time I had met her. She had seen a few men but that does not mean she has jumped into bed with them all either. Remember she was the hardest to seduce of all the women I tried it on with, and I had met quite a few as well but we got to texting and you know what's gonna happen when I text her and she replies. Then ten or fifteen minutes later I get a text that starts *Hi Dr ******* it's ***** was wondering if you had a spare appointment later this week, not just for me but for my step Daughter as well.* Now that is very clever because what will happen is (and this is actually what happened) she drives up to mine and knocks on the door dressed in her suit. I open the door and she tells me she has left Lucy in the car while I examine her

"thats fine" I replied, "pop yourself into my surgery and onto the bed"

At this point I know that she is throbbing expectantly because she knows that I will lift her skirt, put on my gloves, lubricate my fingers and put them high up into her pussy. It's the bit where I lift her skirt and pull her panties to one side that she loves first because within a couple of minutes of knocking on my door she is on her back with her legs open and her little well trimmed pussy is wet and wanton.

The next thrill for her is the sound of the gloves and then the feel of the lubrication on her pussy. You see, it's not always about penetration; it's the build up, the picture you paint, the understanding of the excitement that she will have as all of this unfolds. She orgasms and I tell her that she has no internal damage from her husband's over-physical attacks on her pussy so she thanks me and says she will fetch Lucy. She get's herself together but instead of going to get Lucy she will go into my bedroom where she will change into Lucy.

Now remember the picture would already have been painted through text messages earlier that day or during the week, so we both know what's about to happen. It's not strictly to a script just a general idea. She texted me saying that she thinks Lucy has been having sex with boys in her school so she wants me to examine her and she wants me to teach the little bitch a lesson. She wants me to fuck her hard and spank her and put all sorts of things up into her little pussy to make her climax time and time again. Well say no more lol I think I just may be able to help this lady out. lol

She comes out of my bedroom dressed like a girl from St Trinians and it's very well done indeed; not half way but the whole look. I talk to her as if she was a young woman of seventeen and ask her to get onto the table. As she does she reveals a glimpse of her panties from behind. I tell her to stop and get back down, which she does and I instruct her to bend over. She does this and whilst she is bent over I can see her pussy bulge from the rear.

"Do you know that it is very naughty to show off your pants in front of me?" I ask

"Yes, I do, Doctor," she replied. "My step mum says if I continue to do it the boys might start to do naughty things to me but I haven't told her that they already do. Every dinner time a couple of them are always naughty to me."

I told her that I would have to punish her and she said she was ok with that and asked if it would hurt.

"I am afraid it might, young lady" I tell her. "But it is for your own good."

I part her legs a little and then I spank her bottom; not too hard but enough to make red marks. Then as she is still bent over I pull her panties down, quickly and quite roughly, I move her over to the examination table, push her over it and get my cock out and fuck her very hard. She moans and I could tell she is having an orgasm. I withdraw and let her come down from the orgasm as I get her back onto the table where I use some dildo's on her, then I get out the new one I bought earlier in the week; a big black one with a brown tip. It is eight inches long and actually eight inches in girth. I lube up the new boy, which I have affectionately called the FELLA, and put it against the entrance to her pussy. I slowly move the bell end of the FELLA up and down her lips and nudge it into the entrance, pushing it in just a bit then moving it around again, slowly building up to putting it in all the way. But first I stop at about four inches and pull it back out, not all the way but just to where it matters most. Eventually I let her have it all and she loved it especially when it was all the way up and I was holding a little vibrator on her clit. It was all I could do to keep her on the table and she desperately wanted me to fuck her harder with the dildo, saying, demanding, I do it harder and I did to the point where my wrist was beginning to ache. She came big time and at this point I was ready to fuck her as well so I got her back over the bed and really fucked her for some time. I had a great orgasm and we both just stayed there for what seemed ages, both of us exhausted from the activity. We eventually got it together, had a drink and she went on her way.

Now you may think *Wow, she has got some sex drive* and you would be right but there is more to come because it is not long before she brings the housekeeper, Molly, into the game. So now it is her, the step mother of Lucy and the housekeeper Molly who all need appointments.

Now at this point I am going leave you with your imagination because it won't be hard to work out what happened and it was on a regular basis but then there were the gaps when she would meet someone. Phew! lol

Some will laugh at the next bit; some will wonder what lengths this man will go to for sex. Well let me tell you; great lengths! lol No really, this is more about meeting new women than sex and this is another attempt to find the right lady. So you can picture it; I am on the dating sites, the paid ones, the free ones, I am escorting but not very often, so now I hear that not many men go to the local Salsa classes and the numbers are about ten women per man. Well I had to check it out. I just could not leave all those women without a man to dance with, and a bonus is I learn salsa. lol So I get all togged up and dive in a bottle of aftershave—expensive aftershave I will add—and off I go to the beginners class where I am the only person there. Now the instructor, "a man" seemed a nice bloke but his partner who helped him out was an absolute babe and boy, could she move. So bonus; one-on-one with her might be fun and I have my first half hour learning the basic steps.

Then just as I am coming to the end, The next class comes in and I am being watched by quite a lot of women and the occasional male. I could sense all these eyes checking me out and it felt like my butt was on fire. I have a nice butt; small and firm and a real nice shape, or so I am told. I always say I may have a small nail but I have a quality hammer to knock it in with. lol

The lesson ends and there is a pause before the next lesson starts and I am asked if I would like to join in. I tell them I'm not sure if I should so I ask what the level is like since I don't want to slow the class down.

But really knowing damn right I am staying, Ladies. I need to meet you all. lol Well it's not long before I start to recognise a few women and they are from the dating sites that I am on. There were three in this class that I had recognised and so I wouldn't embarrass them when I got to them in turn during the lesson to reassure them their secret was safe with me and I wouldn't mention here that I had seen them fishing lol, I actually had to explain that to one of them and yes she was blonde. lol And this particular one actually had me down as a favourite on the site so it was a tad embarrassing for her but there you go. lol It was good that I had seen theses three ladies at the dance class because it would save me meeting them on a date lol and none of them were my type anyway. In fact the only ones I liked in the class were too young or they were married so no go there and I don't go there either. I never date or chat a woman up if I know she is married. I know how I would feel so I don't do it, not even if they tell me that they are only still at home because of their kids. I just don't do that sort of thing unless . . . lol There is always an unless, there has to be and this is mine. I mentioned earlier in the book about dating sites. Well there is another less well known site a sister of a fishy one; the naughty one. there are lots of people on there that some people would say, "call very strange" I would say "let them be" if they are doing no harm and they are having fun, if it is okay with them and it does not affect anyone else at all then crack on, people.

Now getting back to married woman; well there are a few, very few, but there are some that need sex that their husband or partner, who they love *mostly*, cannot provide for one reason or another. Now if their husband approaches me or anyone else on the site and wants me to perform with his wife then that is okay by me and if he wishes to watch well then they are both getting something from it; her the sex and him the knowledge that she is getting what he cannot provide, and if it helps them then what's the harm? I always used to say to my younger wife if I ever get too old that I cannot perform you have my permission to get sexual pleasure elsewhere. she told me not to be so stupid that she loved me and could never have sex with anyone else while we were married, SO WHY DID YOU LEAVE ME AND THEN RUN OFF WITH A NORTHERN GAMBLER WHO YOU MET SHORTLY AFTER LEAVING ME? lol lol lol In fact lolling all over my fucking front room two faced cow with double standards, but I loved her and everything about her. FUCKING MUG! I will never, ever let anyone live with me ever again and I will never, ever get married ever again. Unless, and like I said earlier there is always an unless or a but, and this is it for me; they have to be able to support themselves if it all goes wrong. In other words they must own their own property or something similar and they must be willing to sign a pre-nuptial. I would hate myself if I thought I was leaving someone with nothing at all and if I moved in with someone I would want to meet that person halfway with everything; all the costs of the house, all the fuel bills, half the mortgage and half the food. What we own ourselves, like our cars, we meet those costs ourselves as I would be getting a rent from my property and getting my wages and my pension and any other ill-gotten gains. lol So why not? And if they lived with me and rented out their property I would be expecting the same and if we split then I would happily walk away with no claim on that person because I paid my way as we all should do in life and I would expect to be treated in exactly the same way. I am for fairness and justice.

I will tell you just off the top of my head watching a program on TV; Hedge Wars. I have seen similar programmes years ago about the same plant / tree and how some neighbours bully their neighbour or just don't respect their fellow human. Guess what? Give me a call and sometime in the near future you would hear the sound of a chain saw and the crashing of trees and by the time the police arrived I would be well gone but the bullied person would have had justice and fairness, and the bully would be left with the bill to tidy up the mess in their garden. A vigilante, you might say. To that i would say I am not above the law and I would never do anything that would actually cause anyone physical pain, but I like to stand up for those who suffer from injustice. Our current system is a bit dated and there is nowhere near enough flexibility, okay okay okay get off the soap box, I hear you say, and get on with your life after your wife. lol

Well I have flitted from one month to the next and back but it is hard to remember exactly what you did or who you met in the right order and reading this back I sound like I have cheated or been a bit of a tart but honestly I have not. Like I keep saying I never went with anyone else when I was seeing someone.

Life isn't always a bed of roses when you're married. You go through times where you hate the bitch so much you remember the old fashioned Saturday afternoons when, before the football scores, there was the wrestling. I am always remembering Jackie Pallo and Mick Mc Manus, when one or the other would grab hold of the top rope of the ring and do a two-footed drop kick. Well following my ex down the stairs one day I was so fucking angry I could see myself with one hand on the banister and drop kicking the bitch in the back of the head. But I was, of course, only thinking of it and if it were ever to happen I would probably miss and break my spine when landing. lol

Well a few days ago I had another bad day. I don't know what it is. It's like I have not grieved the death of my marriage and it seems like I can't let go. I well up just at the thought of not being liked or wanted and this time I had it so bad that I could not go out because my eyes were so red with the stinging. I went to the shops and on my way back in my truck I felt so low that I found it hard to not cry although tears were running down my face and I could not have managed to speak to anyone if I had to.

I remember getting out of the truck and into my house quickly just in case someone came along. I sat in my front room again wondering how I got here and why I am suffering. Why is it that when men end up with the child it is so hard to get the money? I had just lost my job but was not entitled to any Jobseeker's Allowance because I have a pension. Fuck me, I have paid in all my life and I am not entitled to anything and I am a single man with a ten-year-old boy. My ex is not working so she does not have to pay maintenance, I am not working so I cannot claim any credits other than child benefit and tax credits, but it will take about two months for that to come through as my son has only lived with me for the last two months. It seems so unfair that I have to struggle, yet I have never missed a maintenance payment in my life. I have worked all my life and have paid all my taxes all my life and when I need help for the first time at the age of 55 I am refused so here I am bringing up my son, trying to pay a mortgage and all the bills, food clothes etc and I am trying to live off of my 500 quid a month pension. Yep, its tight; so tight I feel like I am fighting a losing battle. I am down, so far down that I find it easy to cry but to everyone else I put on a front, a funny, happy-go-lucky front. I am sure you can picture it from what I have told you about myself.

I have started to look for more work and managed to get sixteen hours a week at six quid an hour and I won't get paid for five weeks, but it brings me into the working tax credit bracket for a claim so I have applied but have been told it will be at least six weeks before I will receive any money. So I will suffer. Sorry; not suffer because that sounds bad so I will get by. Until then I am trying to get handyman jobs with friends but not wanting to look like I am too desperate I offer my services out and probably a bit too cheap but it has got to be mates' rates as it will not be worth them giving me the work. And I get some good friends to give me some jobs as a favour and I get a whole list of stuff they need doing, but it works out at about three quid an hour less my fuel. So it's not much but it's something and I feel like shit but at the same time I am talking to people, I am getting out there and I am getting rewarded for what I do so I am grateful. The government should be helping genuine people like me and my ex should be paying her way but she would rather not, it seems. She says she can't find work but that's bullshit; I am fifty five and I have always found work. I have had good jobs in the past and now I am cleaning offices and toilets to enable me to shop. If I was an immigrant or a refugee, and sorry to say this, ladies, but it is the way I feel at the moment. If I was a woman I would probably get something. I would be looked after, but instead I am left to get by and struggle and my God, the pressure is bad. Forgive me if I have overstepped the mark people it is just how I feel as I am writing this so it is just me being as honest as I can. My God, how I would love an opportunity to use the skills I have, how I would love to pass on those skills and how I would love to help maybe a small company or even a large company with my knowledge, not just of life but in many areas from manufacturing and production, to plumbing, building and fitting kitchens etc but obviously between the hours of nine am and three pm lol because my son needs his dad to look after him and that I will do.

It's very hard and chokes you up when all your life you have tried to do your best and when it comes to being the person in need you don't get the help or backing I have given in the past to others. It's like a kick in the teeth when you hear that she has gone abroad on holiday twice in the couple of months that my son has been with me and that she is able to not work but keep her savings. That is the money I paid her off with so by not working she does not have to pay me, and because of her savings she does not get Jobseeker's so I could not even get the minimum five quid from her benefits because she has too much money to make a claim. Hey, now I am sounding bitter and twisted and I could have probably put it all in a better way but like I said it is how I feel and it is me being honest.

Of course there may well be a perfectly good reason for her not being able to provide any support for her son. Oh, I forgot to mention that I received this month's child's benefit, but I've not got any child tax credits yet. Don't know what happened to the child benefit for last month or the tax credits or either for the last half of the month before that as well. I cannot help thinking that she has received the benefit; well I know she has but as I have not been given them I will ask the question. I will also ask her for the maintenance I paid her for a month when he was only there for two weeks of that month and that month I was unemployed but I scraped together the money for my son. I used to get very angry and would show my anger outwardly, not through violence but shouting at people and especially to the person who had done me an injustice but now I feel so beaten down that I even put off asking questions that will cause confrontation. I am desperate for an amicable relationship with my ex for the benefit of my son more than anything but I am getting stressed and upset about what she's like

Let's get back on track. lol

Well I met Cornwall lol after a few phone calls and some internet chatting. We met at a popular cafe in the town and had a bit of a giggle and while we did get on I was not as interested as she was, and definitely not as interested as I was initially now that we had met. Why? I ask myself. What is it about me that drives me to meet these really nice people, well mostly nice, lol and then the slightest little thing like a few too many wrinkles or a bit of a belly, even the sound of their voice and other silly things put me off; things that you overlook when you're in love? I don't want to lead people on and I really think that I continue to want to meet these people because I am hoping my feelings will change, but they don't and I do it time and time again, almost in desperation I suppose!!! I can hear people saying I should get a grip; well that's what I think people will be saying. I hope I am not making myself look or sound bad and I do understand that some people will think of me as a player or a complete wanker but hopefully some will be on my wave length and know where I am coming from and hopefully understand me. lol No, that will never happen; no one will understand me! lol

A couple of weeks pass and I contact Cornwall again and we arrange to meet at my house. She comes up the following weekend and I take her out to a small town nearby; very picturesque views over the river and small expensive shops as well as very nice houses where rich people live and great little cafes where a hot chocolate is aboutfour quid. We had a good day; she was fun to be with and quite tactile with a great figure about a size six to eight and about five to seven tall with long curly, blonde hair. She's an an ex model. I say ex but she does do some modelling work now and then.

We get back to mine and we discuss her staying as I cook the evening meal. She says she would like to stay and he would also like to sleep in my bed but not have sex. Well that's a new one on me. lol So I, of course, agree and she stayed the night and yes we slept in the same bed and I did not make any move toward her sexually during the night. In the morning we woke up and lay in bed having a bit of a cuddle. She ran her hands and fingers all over my head, chest, shoulders and arms so I did the same to her, getting closer and closer to her small but very firm boobs and not far from the top of her panties. She told me that she would give me two weeks to pack that in so one thing lead to another and it was not long before I had removed her thong to reveal a very neat little pussy; it was well-shaped with light brown pubic hair.

I started playing as I would usually do and took my time building up to full entry with my fingers. She responded very well and she moved her butt as if she wanted my fingers. I liked the way she did this and I liked the way she was not holding back and the way she moved and enjoyed what was happening. So many women just lie there and are prepared to follow. Not many go with it and enjoy it. She did have a very good orgasm and I let her come down from her climax, just slowly playing with her, then I got on top and entered her. We both enjoyed what was happening and she was a good mover, responded to my movements and speed. We actually both reached an orgasm together which was very good. And what was nice and something I have always liked but does not always happen is that I could feel the vibration and the pulsing and throbbing of her orgasm on my cock. it's not long before we get up and I make breakfast. She gets showered and dressed and we sit and talk in the kitchen; well, she sits and I start to wash dishes and clean up, which is something I never realised I did. Apparently this action of mine to tidy up and organise my house is almost like saying 'okay thanks see ya' lol I never knew that women took it that way until she said. She didn't actually mention it then but she did say it on the phone some time after it happened again the second time so now I am aware of what I do and very conscious that I don't do it with other women.

I made a very good observation the other day whilst food shopping. I noticed it in the shop where I buy most of my food, you know the one in the advert on TV where the women walks away spanking her butt—okay, okay, tapping her pocket but I have a good imagination so she is spanking her butt. Well in that shop there's lots of women walking very quickly with heads down and filling their trolleys fast; that's trolleys as in shopping baskets on wheels and not trolleys as in underpants. I, too, buy most of my stuff from there but spend little time doing it. I have noticed that the shop close to where I live, the one that is almost an anagram for the place where you bury your brains, there seems to be a much better class of women where they walk around very smartly dressed and fit-looking with heads up as if they know they look good. They walk around with a smile on their faces and take their time looking at the goods which is perfect for me because I get time to give them a good check out. Get it?!! lol Also very few have shopping trolleys full up to the brim as they do in the butt-spanking shop, so I spend most of my money and buy most of my food and spend the least amount of time in the butt spanking shop and spend the least money buying the least amount of food but spending most of my time in the place where they bury your brains! lol I have also purposely asked some women some stupid questions about what to buy, or can this be used for such-and-such-a-thing lol just to speak to them and to get eye contact and to know what they sound like. I've never managed to chat anyone up yet but I've got some nice smiles and have always been helped. Maybe it is the way forward; maybe I should try harder at doing this rather than the dating sites and maybe the spanking-your-butt shop and the bury-your-brains shop could be the new MARKET place for dating. lol Sorry; crap attempts at being funny but it makes me smile and that has to be a good thing.

Between dating and mini relationships I had been talking to the wife of an ex-work colleague. They had split and when I started talking to her they were making moves towards divorce, which has since happened. Well we have a lot in common as we both know a lot of the same people and we are both going through divorces. We both have children; well I only have one and she has three, so we are able to relate to each other's emotions. We have met up for a drink and a meal now and again and then always gone back to mine for a last drink and a look on the internet at the social networking sites. We have always been fairly open about what we have both been getting up to; she has always laughed at what she calls my antics and has always said, as many women do, that I don't act or look my age.

Well the last time we met I picked her up and I was a bit early so she invited me in and showed me the decorating she had been doing in the kitchen. Then she was telling me about how she had been to a beer festival that afternoon and was feeling tipsy already. I told her she was looking good and I liked her dress. Mind you, she always looks good. She is very attractive and still only in her late thirties and she has a great body, although she says she has put on a bit around the middle but I couldn't see where. She was wearing a long summery dress that showed a fair amount of her cleavage and I was not complaining; after all she was going out with me that night. Pity it was not a date lol but good for the ego nevertheless As it always is when you're out with a good-looking well-dressed woman. She made a remark about my wardrobe and about it being all in order and she said I ought to look at hers and come around to sort it out for her. Naturally I assured her it would be my pleasure and it would be. lol

Well she finished off last touches to her makeup and we left Driving back to mine we get into conversation about the last dates we both went on and what we both did and she was very open, as I always am, so we talked freely about the naughty bits; not in detail but enough said. lol I am probably a bit too detailed when I talk about it but that's me. So we get back to mine and park the van then walk down to the local eatery. We had a few drinks whilst waiting for our table until eventually we are seated and order our food. Ss she is sat opposite me I could see her cleavage and at times she would lean forward revealing rather more. lol Not that I was complaining at all and the more she relaxed the more often she revealed her cleavage and the less she would adjust her dress which was also good for me but being the perfect gentleman I did point it out at one point. We giggled a lot about what we had been up to and we were having a great time talking about our pasts and swapping information about our present situations, talking about our children and schooling. We used to cover just about everything.

It seems that I have quite a few very good friends and that they happen to be female but that's me. They all know about the female friends I have and we are all happy with things the way they are though if any of my friends was not happy then I would listen to what they had to say and do my best to make them happy by doing whatever it takes—and I am not referring to sex here as all they all mean more to me than an hour of pleasure. They are not sex objects but real people with real feelings. So back off the soap box! lol I seem to jump on that quite often so I must carry it around with me like a politician. lol

Anyway we pay the bill and I always leave a tip; the staff all know me as I eat their very often, and they all know my name but they are very good because they don't let on if I am with a woman they don't recognise. We start back to mine and its only a short walk which seems to take a long time when you've had a few. We get back to mine and I offer her a drink which she accepts then we then sit on one of the two two-seaters I have in my front room known as love seats. They are great and come from a well known company; you know what comes ****. lol We are both looking at my laptop on a social network site and laughing about certain things on there. We do this for about an hour when out of the blue I turn and kiss her.

Oh my God! I've overstepped the mark is the first thing that goes through my mind for the first few seconds.

Will she get up and tell me this is not what she wants or will it be okay and we'll go with the flow?

Well thank God it was okay and we went with the flow. I kissed her for a while before moving my hand to her breast and it's not long before we have settled into the chair and we're kissing passionately. I then do the brave bit; THE BRAVE BIT? I hear you ask, because some or most men think the brave bit is the initial kiss whereas the actual brave bit is stopping the kiss and getting up, taking her hand and suggesting we go somewhere more comfortable, You see, a kiss is a kiss and it's easy to stop kissing; nothing lost by kissing someone. But to move on to the bedroom is a different thing altogether. This is where you are both about to reveal all there is to reveal with nothing left to the imagination, especially if you have known each other, as we had, for about twenty years. I was even at her wedding. So what happens next can make or break the relationship we have and what I mean by relationship is, because there are different types of relationships, nothing after this next hour or so is ever going to be the same. Will we still be friends? Are we both okay with what is about to happen? This is different from all the other relationships for reasons I have already covered,

Well we did enjoy ourselves and we had sex in many positions. We played with my toys; well one of them but not the Fella. lol She had very firm boobs and they were a perfect size for me as I am not particularly a boob man. Don't get me wrong; I do love them but I'm not obsessed with size. She had sensitive nipples and they were very erect when I played with them and she enjoyed it very much when they were in my mouth and being flicked with my tongue.

I worked my way down to her pussy which was shaped and close-cut and very neat with full and firm lips and a very nice clit, which I sucked and licked. She was definitely liking what was happening. I first entered her in the missionary position and we both moved around putting equal effort into enjoying the moment. Then I moved away, putting her into the position I call the bookkeeper and we did this for a while until I suggested we use the dildo. She was game, which pleased me, so I got it out of the drawer and lubbed it up but when I went to use it she jumped back a bit and said it was cold. I should have known better really as I usually warm them up in hot water first, so I stopped and warmed it up in hot water and when we restarted it was much better as it was more realistic since it was warmer and softer from the heat of the water and the slipperiness of the lubrication.

I played with this for some time and with great results because she moved very well. It was very sexual for me to see someone enjoying me playing with my toy and it was not long before she had her first orgasm. I then put her on all fours and took her from behind while we alternated from hard to long slow strokes until we both came again. It was a very good night and I would hope it would happen again. To this day we are still very good friends and we still contact each other quite often but as yet have not had a repeat performance. lol It may or may not happen again and if it does I am sure we will do it for fun. If it does not happen then I am sure we will still be great friends for a very long time.

Let's get back to the dating sites. I have just remembered a funny story which is all true so I will tell it as it happened. As usual I am trawling the free dating sites which is atwice daily ritual for me, I say that but at the moment I am not actually on any of the sites so it *was* a ritual but not anymore. Well I start to chat to another lady from the darkest depths; lol you know, Cornwall. lol She lives in a small town about an hour away from where I live and we get around to setting up a meet. I agree to drive down so it's a Friday night meet and she has given me directions so off I set down the winding lanes, getting deeper into banjo country where you need eyes in the back of your ass as well as your head. lol You've seen the film "Deliverance" Well this is not far off! lol

Seriously it's a beautiful drive in the best part of the UK. Well second best. The best is where I live. lol I get to the exact road which is a cul-de-sac so I park at the entrance to it. I didn't know exactly where she lived so I texted her to say that I had arrived in the location agreed and she replied that she would be there in a moment I looked in my rear view mirror and I see a woman approaching. she looked nice, about a size twelve-ish nicely dressed in a short dress showing her shapely legs so I step out of the truck lol and wait for her to approach. We go through the regular compliments and I ask her to lead the way to where she would like to have a drink so we start walking up through the picturesque village and get to a main road. Well it had a few cars on it so it would be their main road. lol As we get to the kerb and are about to cross she stops and waves at a car on the main road.

"That's my daughter," she says.

Woaaaah! I was thinking *she was fit* but luckily what came out was "Oh. She obviously takes after her mother; very pretty," I said and smiled knowingly.

I say knowingly; that is she knew it was bullshit and I knew she knew. lol So we crossed the road and entered a very nice pub and I went to the bar and ordered a drink and I will say straight away she did offer and she did buy the next one so she was a good girl. lol We sat down and chatted and I found I actually liked her and she was a fit-looking woman with a decent figure. She showed more and more of her leg as she relaxed. I sat next to her on the couch and it was not long before I began to look into her eyes and touch her, firstly during conversation on her arm and leg and then as the drinks went down I put my hand on her shoulder as my elbow was on the back of the couch. I was basically resting my arm but opening my body up to her. She was facing me but sat next to me, also opening her body up, which told me she was relaxed and comfortable and that she liked where she was at that time. In other words she liked me and was enjoying her time in the pub. It was'nt long before I started to touch her hair, just the odd time while my hand was on her shoulder and I could see she liked this.

We swapped a few stories about previous experiences of dating and we both talked about our work and families, the usual stuff; just outlines and headlines with no real detail because that comes with time.

I am always aware of talking too much and of talking over people. I always make sure I let them tell their stories and I listen well. And at times I will relate to something and respond with a similar anecdote but you have to watch it because you don't want to come over as having blacker cat, even though you are genuine and you really have had the same or a similar experience. so we are getting on really well but a spanner in the works—well actually a small tool box really—was a couple of things came out over a few minutes which caused me to have a rethink; a revaluation of the night so far and what I was actually thinking was a reality check. The thing is she dropped in that she was only renting and that she had two daughters and one lived with her. Well that bit was okay until she said that she would not leave the area or consider moving in with anyone until her daughter had decided to leave home herself. That was ok too but that would mean I would have to drive an hour each way to see her every time.

So she has commitments and she is renting. Well I carry on as if not disturbed by this as I did not want to spoil the evening so we finish our drinks and I walk her back to her flat which was only about hundred yards past where the truck was parked. We stopped at the main entrance to her block and we chatted for a while until eventually I go in for the first kiss. I'm not sure why really becauseI had already decided that I would not be coming back again. But hey, I am only human, I'd had a few Stellas. She was looking good and she was up for it as well and she may be thinking the same as me so get in there, my son! lol,

Well the kiss gets a little passionate and I ran my hands over her boobs and did all the usual stuff and there was no pulling away so I went for the big one and ran my hand down her hip and across to her pussy. Obviously we are outside her door so it was outside of her dress. She let me for a while but as I got to the point of getting my hand up her dress then she pulled away a bit which meant don't go there; yet. lol So I brought my hands around to the back of her dress and onto her butt. *Fuck me!* was my first thought as this butt looked great in the dress but it felt like a half empty airbag when I groped it. Not good; not good at all. I know I'm fussy but that's me. There are things about me that some women won't like but I can live with that. I can deal with it in my mind and I don't hold it against them. Like I have said beauty is in the eye of the beholder and we all see different aspects of the same person. We actually hear different meanings from the same words said too, and we can all read different things into the same written message or note. If more people had the same outlook as me lol we would all get on a lot better.

You must first and foremost appreciate that we all have our beliefs and points of view and that we are entitled to them. I don't believe in religion but I don't think that people who do are fools; I just think it is their choice. I am not going to sugest that a particular person is a bible puncher because I can't be doing with all that so I will not have anything to do with them. Far from it; I have many friends who are religious, who are black, who are disabled, who are not too bright, who are ugly, who are pretty, who are fat, who are skinny, who are geniuses and who are short. lol I think you get the idea lol Got to get off of my soap box again! Lol.

Well we are still kissing when the door opens. She pulls back quickly as her youngest daughter walks out and it is obvious what mother was doing; yes, she was kissing this strange man outside the front door of her flat. Well at this point I decide to make my excuse and leave so we have a quick peck on the cheek and I say goodnight. Walking back toward the van I have made the decision that in the morning I will text her and let her know that it was not to be and we will both move on.

I need to explain about my present circumstances. It may or may not answer some questions you may or may not have since lol you are forming an opinion of me and I hope it is a good one.

When my wife actually left me, which was about two months after she told me, she moved into a flat nearby. She carried on working at the same company I originally worked for and we shared the custody of my youngest son, our son, as I have two older ones from a previous marriage. When I say shared what was really happening was she was so involved with her new man friend and going to see him up north that I ended up having much more time with my son than her. Eventually she introduced my son to her new man. Now this really annoyed me; not that she was introducing him but the way she actually did it because it was with very little thought to my son's feelings and his thoughts about what is happening.

This is how she did it; she had been away for a few days in the north visiting her chap and they flew back together. She then drove to mine with him in the car and knocked on my door as arranged to pick up my son. I never knew at this time that her new man would be in her car outside of my house. I don't have an issue with him at all as he never stole her from me as far as I could see at that point but I was fuming that she was going to introduce her new man to my son outside my house and in the back of her car. WHAT THE FUCK WAS SHE THINKING? Obviously with no thought or consideration to my son OR me come to that. WHAT A FUCKING BITCH? okay back to normal now! lol But that incident has played on my mind over and over; of how my son must have felt. It was not long after that when she took my son on holiday to the north where this man lived. I have to say I went there on a date once, a little while after he moved there, and found it to be very disappointing. I am not a snob but the Metro Centre—OOOPS, that's given it away lol—is like a giant cheap shop and most of the people were walking around in tracky bottoms and leopard skin dresses. So chav and so, so, so cheap looking. It was a let's-buy-and-live-for-now mentality. Nothing wrong with the north or any people that come from there I have many friends from that part of the country but it was definitely the impression I was getting, Eventually, about a week later, she came back and when she came around with my son she said she was moving to his place up north and that she was taking my son with her. It was against my wishes but we did agree that if he did not like it that he would be allowed back to live with me after giving it a fair try.

Obviously I was devastated because we did so much together and it would be a massive chunk out of my life. Needless to say my ex and I had many, many discussions and arguments and things were said out of anger on both sides but we eventually came to a decision and we agreed he would come back if he wanted to. So I paid her every month; never missed and I sent her extra if he had anything special to do. I sent extra to her for him for a new game etc; I bought him clothes when he was down with me on visits to see him I had to drive a hundred and twenty miles to an airport and park my van overnight at thirty five quid a time. I also had to wait overnight in the airport, where it was £3:50 for a coffee, until seven am the following morning each time then fly him back. She would drive down with her fella and pick him up in her brand new hatchback, usually staying overnight at her mum's and driving back the next day or staying the night then picking him up in the morning and driving back.

Eventually my son asked to come back and of course she said no that was not going happen but he kept on and eventually she gave in. Not that she had any choice because I said that I would come up and pick him up and it was his choice by law where he wanted to be. You see eventually, after the silly people had paid lots to solicitors for their work and court appearances, it all boils down to a court recognised association to do a case study ending with what the child really wants to do, so cutting out all the grabbers, leaches and anyone else who wants to make an easy dollar this is how it really works. If your child is old enough to make up his mind where he really wants to be and if there is no difference between the two places he could be, then his choice is granted. So he would pick me and I could offer the same or more than his mother so it would be me he comes to. But it would have cost about £5000 but for free we discussed it like grown adults and let my son decide after knowing all the facts. That's what I call being sensible. Obviously I may or may not have made it sound correct but I am sure we all understand what I am saying. If you don't or you don't believe me then dig a bit and ask the questions. Don't pull any punches and you will be enlightened by the truth.

I had to wait though because I could not get him a school place in the school that he'd left until the September so in the August I picked him up. All of his stuff was outside, including him although she did come out to say goodbye to him but I was disgusted with the cold way in which it was done. Just like the way he'd met her new man. She is so cold and I can't believe she has changed so much.

We get home and while he was away I had decorated his room to how he would like it and when we get in he is so pleased and happy. And I can tell you now he is so happy to this day. We go out at least five times a week after he has finished playing with his mates at the park and we have had tea. We go for a walk and he takes his scooter and we chat as he plays and he really lets go. And our discussions are very much instigated by him which is what I want. I don't want it to be like I'm searching for information as if he was being questioned.

It has taken two months and he comes out with stuff that shocks me even now, but we are happy and he is happy with life. We have a great understanding but we have boundaries and rules and he knows them and appreciates them, although I do tend to be more relaxed than I should be but I will tighten it up as time passes.

He is very good at school; sorry, he is actually excellent at school and in the top couple of percent in all subjects and leading the way in maths. I try to encourage as many activities as I can because he has a tendency to put on weight but all in all he is happy and I am happy he is with me, though I will say I am not happy with certain things in my life.

My ex does not pay any kind of maintenance at all. She is out of work since moving up north over a year ago. She gives my son £10 a month pocket money which she pays into the bank account I opened for him. I put in £20 a month and I am fairly strict with his bank money as he must learn to control money so he needs to work to earn it. If he does well then he gets a bonus and I do set him incentives like distance on his mountain bike. All the incentives I use are exercise or educational so he gets rewarded for doing well in the things that count. I know I am rambling on here and I am very much aware that some people may switch off when I get away from the sex and the escorting or dating but remember this is informative as well and you can take the relevant info from what I say out and use it to suit your needs. It does not just apply to men but to women just as much and while I have written this as a man because I am a man it still works both ways.

I know of many men who are right twats when it comes to maintenance or having their children for the weekend or week even. Loads more men run away from their responsibilities than women, but there are some women that do that as well. In an ideal world we should see past the relationship that's falling apart and think about what's best for the children we have first and foremost.

Okay okay I hear you. So a bit about the misbehaving fish in the sea now; you know, the naughty ones. Yes, that site. lol I was shocked when I first went on it and I wondered if it could all be real and if all those women were telling the truth. Or was it just a load of women who get their rocks off from showing and saying naughty things on the internet.

I wrote my profile and a bit about my sexual desires and what I am into and what I am good at; well in my opinion anyway! lol I then signed up for three months at an introductory rate and began to trawl the site. Get it? Trawl?!! lol I could not believe what I was seeing First there were some stunning women of all ages into all sorts of things and when you looked at their profile there would be a distance indicator to show you how far away they were from your post code. You also got an email and site message to tell you that your profile had been viewed. I started to send messages out to various misbehaving fish/women lol and got some replies as well as more pictures from them and there was one that I had recognised from a sister site. We had actually fallen out over as it happens; a misunderstanding about a comment I made and she blocked me from contacting her. But less than two weeks later she comes up in my message box with "Well, what a small world?"

I reply of course and note that the distance was "0" so she lived very close. We swapped messages for a while and she asked how spontaneous I could be. My reply was of course "very" lol Well a week or so had passed without any contact and then I had just pulled up outside my house at 9pm after arriving home from a Salsa class, and as I pulled up the text tone goes off and the message was from her—"fancy being spontaneous?"

Of course my reply was red or white in five minutes? She said red and also gave me her address. I went in and collected a bottle and the phone went again. It was her to say give her twenty minutes so I did and I walked down to her place which was actually only about two hundred yards from mine. I knocked on the door to see for the first time in the flesh the lady I had been chatting to on two different sites. But what is different about this site and this meeting is that it is not about relationships as in potential life partners but about sex; guaranteed sex. You both know why you're meeting and you both know what you're into so no tentative discovery needed.

She opened the door in a black silk dressing gown and asked me in and we went up to her apartment. We chatted for about twenty or thirty minutes although we did not talk about sex or anything like that as we had no need to. We actually had a good conversation about our children and a rough outline, sort of headlines, about ourselves. We were sat on the settee in her front room and I kissed her. We carried on kissing for . . . oh, about thirty seconds lol and she suggested we go into the bedroom where I took off my clothes and she removed her silk gown to reveal more than ample boobs and a fair figure. She was not too tall and not what I would classify as slim but she had a nice little figure. I stood at the side of the bed and she was laid on her front with just her little black panties on and no sooner had I removed my boxers when she reached out for my cock so I moved toward her and she started sucking me off and she was very good at it. I leaned over her and made attempts to touch her up as far as I could from the position we were in. Well after a couple of minutes I joined her on the bed and removed her panties to reveal a thin, trimmed black line of pubic hair and nice full pair of lips and once again a very neat pussy. Her lips were soft and very fleshy and she was very moist already.

It was not long before I had my fingers inside her pussy and I played for some time before taking them out. I moved her onto all fours and pushed my fingers in once more and this time she pushes back onto my fingers, wanting as much as she can get inside her. She orgasmed big time with a very tense body and quite a bit of noise so I reached for my bag where I had my dildos and lubrication. I would not have bothered with lube as she was so wet but I went straight for the biggest one known as the FELLA! lol I mentioned it earlier. She had stayed on all fours so I inserted the Fella and she absolutely loved it and it was all I could do to hold it in place. Honestly I used this extremely big dildo on her for ages. It was such a long time my arm and wrist were starting to ache. She loved it big time and orgasmed again but I could not resist her rather plump little ass. I'd learned from the profile that she liked a spanking and it was a spanking I gave, not holding back too much like I would from spanking someone I had just met on a straight dating site or trapped on a night out.

Oh I have not mentioned my theory on trapping. I will later and I will also chat about how to date some women who would not normally take any notice but that's later. I spanked her bottom good and hard and there really was my hand print on her butt. She loved it and whilst her ass was still tingling and smarting with the sting of the spank I pushed my cock into her butt and I fucked her hard. After a while I grabbed the smaller of the two dildos I had brought with me and even though it was a struggle I pushed it into her pussy whilst I was still in her little ass. She moaned and got quite vocal about how hard she wanted to be fucked and I did it quite hard, both in her bottom and up her pussy with the dildo. Eventually I stopped using the dildo. The truth is I could not take any more since my wrist was fucking killing me. Honestly, fellas, it's the truth and anyone who says they would have done it all night? Well you're a liar; or you're a better man than me. Which is possible but it's slim. lol

I dropped the dildo and took my cock out of her bottom and put it in her pussy, a bit like throwing a kit bag into a four tonner; army talk. lol But it is surprising how a woman's pussy works. It's a bit like memory foam and it was not long before it remembered it was not meant to be that big but until then it was like fucking fresh air. Oh, I wish I had a big cock at times and I had the feeling so did this little lady. Sorry; did I say little? lol She was only little in height full stop. I gave her the best I had and I banged her hard because that's what she wanted and it lasted for about fifteen minutes or so. Well it felt like an hour. You know, ladies; like to us men three inches seems like six and one hour seems like half a day. But I did cum and so did she and once again I experienced my favourite thing; I could feel her pussy pulsing almost as if it was sucking onto my cock it is a very nice feeling and I am probably not explaining how nice it actually is.

We stopped for a while and whilst I sat on the floor she laid face down on the bed looking at me over the edge. We were both naked and drinking our wine whilst having a pleasant discussion about family life and what we have both been up to on various sites. I suppose about thirty minutes passed and I stood up and thought to myself I was actually going to leave here without a complaint about stamina or the feeling that I had not given a 100% so I went around the other side of the bed and ran my hands around her waist and bottom and then opened her legs. It was not long before I was very hard again and so I start to take her in the bookkeeper's position. I held her down firmly and banged her very hard, the thrust being absorbed by her ample butt and the fleshy back of her thigh's which wobbled sexily as I thrust my cock in. I did this for a while and she was enjoying it and moving around very nicely then all of a sudden, out of the blue, came the demand "FIST ME!"

Well I nearly dropped through the floor! I withdrew and she got on all fours. Now I have never done this before and to be honest I was not okay about doing it now. Some may ask why, Well for a start I have a big fist. lolling lol lol Sorry, I did not mean to laugh then, but it's true and I had already given her four fingers that night, I also found it quite stomach churning that I was about to ram my fist up a woman's pussy, I remember seeing it in a film before but what I saw was an old fashioned way of dealing with an unfaithful wife/partner which also ended in death and that picture has remained with me, so I am sorry to say I FAILED! Yes, FAILED! OMG what will become of me? lol

I carried on with the best part of my hand until she had an orgasm, and believe me I wanted to be out of there by this time, I'd had enough of sex for one night and not surprisingly either as it was now 01:45 so we had been at it for a couple of hours and a bit more. Oh, I still see her to talk to and we swap texts and messages on FB and if the opportunity came up for being spontaneous with her again I would jump at it and may even fist the lady. lol

Got this on my phone just now.

Four Mates plan a camping trip, two days before they go Paddy's wife tells him he aint going, of course his mates are all disappointed but still decide to go on without him anyway, it's two days later when paddy's three mates arrive at the camp site to find paddy sitting outside his tent all set up and having a BBQ, "how did you persuade the wife to let you come", well Paddy says I was sat in my chair watching the telly when she walked in wearing a see though nightie and crotch less panties, she led me upstairs and then she laid on the bed and handcuffed herself to the headboard and closed her eyes, and then she said "DO WHAT EVER YOU WANT" so here I am.

Just thought I would share that with you because it made me laugh when I needed to.

I'd had a bad few days and I'd actually stood in the cleaning cupboard at work today and could not leave until I knew my eyes were looking okay. I keep getting right downers when I think how much I have had and have lost and about how I am going to get past all this. it was the second time today of four so a really bad day and I do understand that it is like feeling sorry for yourself. You know you shouldn't but you can't stop yourself. Believe me it has taken some balls to write this as I am not the type of person to admit that I am down and when people read this book, assuming it is good enough and I get it published I will have issues with revealing who I am but that's a decision some way ahead and I will make that when the time comes.

Oh, and don't lend this book to anyone; I need to sell as many as I can! lol

You remember when the ex first left and I said I went on a spending spree? lol Well it was great at the time but not that sensible really because now I have lots of stuff, clothes etc, and my son has everything he needs like laptop, mountain bike, BMX, scooter, skateboard etc, So why do I do it? Well it's time to explain a little about my childhood. I never had a bike until I was about thirteen and I bought that from the paper round wages. I remember it cost me ten bob; that's 50p in new money. lol Now that does not seem a lot but in those days it was a fair amount. I had to deliver papers for two weeks for it and okay, it was second hand and only had one brake but the three speed gears worked fine and there was tread on the tyres. And I remember painting it red. lol

I was the middle of three children. I had a younger sister and an older brother and he was Dad's favourite out of us boys. He also sucked up to my dad, trying his best to please him, and because my sister was four years younger she was always going be treated ok. Me? Well I'm not saying this to make you feel for me because I don't need to but I was the black sheep, always in trouble, never at school and that's a shame because now I know I had loads of ability but never used it. I now understand why I was so naughty; I believe that I was trying to be noticed but the trouble was I was getting noticed for all the wrong reasons. I am still like this in a way because I do things to get noticed and to get a reaction like a shock or a laugh, but I am not naughty. lol I will say stuff that's true to certain people and they will be shocked at what I do or say and I will also dress in a way that is way over the top for where I am or what I am doing. Don't get me wrong; I am not dressed up when I am working or anything like that but when I go shopping I will probably be dressed quite smart but in a way that will get attention. Like I will wear a powder blue and white striped shirt with a pair of flashy jeans as well as powder blue trainers with stripes to match my jeans. Instead of the shirt I may wear a powder blue jumper; now that's slightly over the top to shop at the butt spankers! lol I have quite a few jumpers, all v-neck and mostly pastel colours and I have trainers that more or less match them all, I even go as far as to pick jeans with the right coloured stitching; not many people would notice that jeans have different coloured stitching. All my jeans are in shade order in my wardrobe as are all my clothes lol and my hair will be perfect. lol I will have moisturiser on, not too much, but it gives your skin a nice shine and makes you look healthy. I also use tinted moisturiser sometimes to give a better look and tone down the red in my cheeks and I will also have a real nice aftershave on as well. But after the look comes that air of confidence that I portray when walking around and looking. Is it a show? Well yes, it is really but I like to do it and it is me; it's part of who I am.

I went out to a well known dating site's dance at a hotel in the city centre. It was the first time the dating site had held a dance in this city so I arranged to meet one of my female friends outside. It was the very pretty one that liked me as a Doctor, Now this move will be seen as bad by some and good by others. Why? Well because I am walking into a dance full of single women with a stunner. lol STUPID! I hear you shout. Anyway, I am dressed in a mid-grey shiny suit with no jacket since as I think I said before I hardly ever wear a one, The suit was not too shiny like the ones from the eighties but shiny nevertheless, with it I wore a medium to dark purple and white striped shiny shirt, a modern one with a very nice set-back front to the collar. The stripes were mostly different widths. Purple with white ones between them, the shirt looked great with the suit. I always have the waistcoats tailored to fit so it looked great with my body shape so you can picture me walking into this hotel with a very well-dressed and stunning blonde to a singles night. lol

I got what I expected and wanted. Everybody was looking because everyone else was dressed casually; you know, smart-ish, and they looked fine. In fact some looked great, as I would in my jeans and T-shirt lol but I like to be different. The women were all dressed smarter than all the men, as they always do; well except me; Women love to get dressed up and go out and some like to do it more often than others but mostly all women like to dress to impress. Men like to give the laid back I-am—okay-with-how-I-am impression. The-take-me-as-I am attitude and that's great as well but just not for me.

Oh, I forgot to mention that I have my hair cut every four weeks by a man who has won many competitions for men's styling and I also have my nails done sometimes. lol I would like my teeth done but can't afford it and I hate my teeth. I'd had a little work done on my nose many years ago but it needs more and I wear contacts. I know all this sounds a bit much and some may say vain but I am not at all. I just like to look good or should I say the best I can with what I have. I know a good looking bloke when I see one and you don't have to be gay to recognise that a man is good looking. Lads, just get real and relax.

I am meeting a lady at a well known ski slope that has a bar. The slope has been here for a few years now and is well known in the county but although it is not far from my house I have hardly used the bar or the slope. The lady I am meeting is GOK and I talked a little about her earlier. Well we're meeting for the first time after talking online for a couple of weeks and we both arrived in the car park at more or less the same time so I went over to meet her at her car. We exchanged the usual pleasantries and walked to the bar where I bought us both a drink and before we go any further I've got to say here that yep, she bought the next round. Good girl; very good girl. lol Well we chatted for about an hour and it became obvious that we were not each other's type. I talked about myself and my escorting stuff and about some of the funny dates I had been on and about my life in brief, obviously, and she did the same. She said that I had sexy eyes and I have been told that before but I think they are piggy eyes. But hey, I was not going to turn down a compliment. I think it is because I have long lashes. She also said that I dressed well and we then started talking about dress sense and how colours and style match your complexion and shape. She was intrigued by how I knew so much about woman's shapes and about matching colour to complexion and shape and about what you should or should not wear together. We also talked about women and what they think or how they think and about body language and what turns women on and about the body of a woman. She asked how I knew so much; well I pay attention, that's how. I listen to what they say. Yes, I LISTEN, lads. Maybe you should do more of that since LISTENING is a skill that unlocks many drawers . . . sorry doors! lol Well we finished our drinks and it had been about two hours or so then we made our way back to the car park. I walked her to near where her car was parked and we both agreed at that point that we were not each other's type but it had been a fun evening and we would keep in contact which usually means see ya and never chat ever again. lol Now I know what you're thinking; all that chat, you got on well and you took her to her car in the car park. You were all waiting for me to say I fucked her in the truck or something, weren't you? Well keep reading. lol It may well happen.

About two weeks later I get a call from Gok. She says she is off to a sporting event in Cardiff with her company and she's not too sure what to wear and could I help her out. because the type that will help anyone I agreed and told her to grab some of the clothes she liked in her wardrobe then go shopping and grab clothes that she would like to wear. Not sure about from loads of shops but if they are no good she can always return them. I told her to bring her clothes over to mine and we would have a fashion show and I would take pics of how she looked in each outfit and between us we could mix and match till we get the right look for her.

So the following week she turns up at mine with loads of clothes with her so she comes in and we start with a glass of wine just to relax as we chat about the event she is attending, It is a sporting event in Wales but it is not rugby; it has something to do with vision and a ball. lol Well she eventually starts to take off her top to try one of many tops on. Now she is certainly not shy because she stripped down to her bra without embarrassment and I had only met her for two hours once a couple of weeks ago, Now to say she had big boobs would be an understatement. She had more than a handful; actually more than a few handfuls. lol She then went into my bedroom to change her dress and came out to show me. I took pictures and we discussed the good and bad about what she had on and I showed her the pictures so she could see the difference. It was not long before she needed to remove her bra which she did a bit shyly at first but she did do it without any input from me.

Now I was not sexually turned on by her being topless at all. As I have said boobs don't do it for me but I have the time to explain the situation in the book in order o paint a picture for you to imagine Here we have a lady who is not really, fat, but not skinny by any stretch of the imagination. She is taller than average and about a sixteen to eighteen dress size. She is an attractive dark blonde, with a nice personality, and what's sexy about the situation is that she is taking her clothes off in front of me and talking openly about her clothes and body, not the fact that she has her very full naked boobs just inches away. lol Do you get the picture? lol So I now feel like she actually wants me to kiss her. Now if she had said or even says now that she does not want, nor did she want, anything more than just friendship and I mean friends not friends with benefits, then I would be very happy to just do that but even happier to take it further and have sex. I would not think any less of her for saying no and I really mean that because I can deal with topless or almost naked women around me without having to have sex thereby thinking of them as just sex objects. I am a man but I am also in control of my actions and thoughts and I have respect for people and how they feel and their thoughts.

She is standing in front of the full length mirror wardrobe door in my bedroom and I reach over and kiss her gently on the lips. She responds and we have a bit of a snog. Now she is already topless so I start on her nipples and also caressing her very large, full boobs. Her nipples are very hard and erect and I go down on them, licking, flicking and sucking and she is enjoying it very much. since I am almost on my knees as I play with her boobs I am in a great position to pull her panties down and reveal a natural but close-trimmed light brown pussy. It is another very neat pussy. I seem to be having luck in the neat pussy department; not that there is anything wrong with the not-so-neat ones. lol I work my way up to her neck and lips with my mouth and back go to kissing her again and at this point I am standing up straight and the middle finger on my left hand slides down and into the slit between the close-cut but very full lips. I separate her lips by sliding two finger down between them, one each side of her clit and I am doing this with just enough pressure to part them and I can feel her open her legs more inviting me in. I increase my pressure and speed up the rubbing of her pussy lips and clit; she is getting wet and I assist this by sliding my middle finger deep under her to the entrance of her pussy where she is very wet. I lubricate my finger with her juices and then slide my fingers back up so I am lubricating her clit and the inside of her full lips.

I guide her back to lay on the bed and whilst she lays on her back I open her legs a fair way and now with my right hand I part her lips with my two outer fingers, holding them open wide and use my two middle fingers to play with her clit. She likes this very much and has a great orgasm then I slow down my movements and move around to the front of her and pick her legs up, bringing her knees up to her boobs thereby more or less revealing all of her pussy and it was a very red, pink and wet pussy, I go down on her, pushing my tongue as far in as possible and also parting her lips and sucking her clit with just a gentle nibble and she absolutely loved that, I stand up and slide two fingers inside her but only as far as the sensitive entrance where the hymen would have been when she was a virgin.

I have noticed that women love this area being played with, just as if you were putting your cock in part way just to the point where it breaks through. I play here for a while then let her legs down and I eventually mount her, sliding my cock in and fucking her slowly. She moves with excitement and is obviously enjoying it all so I ask her if she would like to try a dildo.

"Why not?" she replies.

From previous conversations we'd had I know she had never used one on herself before so I go and get the biggest one and lubricate it very well, I then hold the tip of it around her pussy; sliding it up and down her lips and around the entrance to her love canal. lol Each time I bring it near the entrance I push it in a little bit and each time it is a bit more and eventually she is attempting to mount the Fella as I lovingly call it. She is well up for it now so once the thick tip of the Fella had past the point of no return I slowly work it in and out more each time until she eventually has the whole dildo right up inside her and I am also playing with her clit and at times even sucking and flicking her nipples with my tongue. She is moving well and for a large lady she is very up for it so I turn her on her side into the position I call the bookkeeper and I know she has not had anal sex before so I am on my knees and thrusting the Fella into her pussy at a fair speed and at the same time I start to move my bell end around her bottom hole. She is well aware of what is happening and each time I put it in the right place to push it in she says yes, and so I start to push it in. She is very turned on and as I push my cock deep into her bottom she orgasms spectacularly

I slowly remove the dildo and let it drop to the floor then I hold her leg up and bang her bottom with some hard strokes. She loves it so I try to stay in her whilst I get her onto all fours. It's a bit awkward but I managed it then I grab her hips and fuck her bottom quite hard. I do not want to come in her so I withdraw and put it in her pussy. I must say I fucked her for at least another ten minutes, which may not seem long but to get fucked hard for that time takes it out of the pair of you. I eventually came and I just stood behind her for a while, getting myself together, until eventually I pulled out actually about a second before it fell out as it was on its way to being soft again. lol

We laid on the bed for a while and chatted and she started us giggling by immediately asking me how much that was lol

"Eh?" I say

"Well if I was paying how much would that have been?" she asked, giggling as she said it.

Well you didn't take me for a meal or a drink so it was straight into the sex," I said. "So I get paid £150 an hour, that was about forty five minutes so call it £120 with the tip included."

We were both laughing quite a lot by this time and eventually she started talking about her fantasies and how she had not ever managed to fulfil them and the reason for that being is she had never told anyone what they were.

I asked her about her marriage and if they ever talked about sex during sex or at any other time and she said that they had, but they had never really ever discussed their real desires. From talking to so many women I find that quite common. It's quite funny how so many women are very knowledgeable and up for most things and are well experienced. Then there are some at the other end of the scale, they are willing but never have, so ladies, if you're someone who has still not tried out your desires use this as a wake-up call and throw any inhibitions you may have in the bin, get down and get dirty. lol Honestly, you need to do what you really want to do and it will be everything for some and not quite everything for others but whatever it is get on and do it. And if you need any help I will be putting a contact email address at the end of the book and will do my level best to answer all questions that I can and I mean I will answer. If you don't get a reply it is because I hope that there is too many. If that's the case I have sold many books. lol And hey, if you send a picture and your my type? Hell, we may even have a date. I am still single and I am still looking, and you have a great advantage; you know all about me.

So sorry; back to Gok. Lol Well she confessed to me that she has never told anyone her real fantasy as she feels that they will laugh at her or think she is weird and a lot of people, both men and women, never say what they feel for precicely those reasons and because they don't want to be seen as some sort of depraved sex maniac or a pervert. But it is not like we have'nt all had fantasies and believe it or not most are very similar. You may feel like it is strange but that's because you have probably never really discussed the subject.

This particular lady wants to be tied up and punished sexually by someone in a combat uniform as if she was taken prisoner by an invading force. Well you can imagine the scenario. I asked her then about the things she would like to happen and of course she was still a bit shy about telling me so I mentioned all the usual things. I painted a picture for her in her mind where a soldier dressed in combats comes in, ties her to her bed and partially blind folds her for a while so she can see what is about to happen. She sees him getting dildos out and she also catches a glimpse of him undoing his combat trousers and the bulge in his boxers. He reaches over and pulls the blindfold down so she cannot see anything and on her wish list are spanking, her butt as well as her pussy, fairly rough handling of her pussy and boobs, anal sex, oral sex, pulled around into various positions, held down, handcuffed, hair pulling and she also has the desire to be fucked outside in a place where she may be seen.

I suggest that she is taken out to a remote spot and bent over a rock or a fallen tree log, secured in a position where she could not do anything to stop anybody from having sex with her from behind, her skirt lifted up over her butt and her panties removed. She would then be blindfolded and left to her imagination. Would it be me taking her from behind or some stranger that happened along? Or possibly even a friend I had roped in. She would not know and she thoroughly loved this idea.

I will definately say right now that I would not ever let someone be that vulnerable for real and I would always be nearby but obviously silent and it would be me taking her; no one else and I would not involve anyone else either unless I was asked to by the woman as that would be a total violation of that woman's rights as a person and a female. Only a low life would ever carry out such a thing.

After talking to many women I have also realised that some not many ladies but some have never really taken notice or even seen other women naked. Now this may seem strange but it is very true. It is also true that not many women actually know what men like in a woman's body. lol I hear you laughing and saying *"Of course we do ya pratt! All men like boobs, all men like pussy, some men like big boobs, some men like big women and some like small women and small butts."* Yes, lol that is all true, but let's get down to basics. What is it that men really like when they get down to a woman's bits? Well sorry for sounding basic but this is very true. When you're at a beach or on holiday all men, or most anyway will check you out; not just your general figure and your face but your boobs, your butt and your pussy. What are they looking for? Well most men like big boobs. Me? I am not too fussy about boob size and most men like a nice small firm butt, as I do, and also most men like a pussy that has a bulge, which is something I like too, Some men like a clean shaven, smooth pussy and if that has a bulge then all the better. Some like it natural; full hair but shaped, and some like it natural shaped and trimmed thin but mostly men like a pussy that is neat to look at and with a nice bulge.

When a woman is bent over, for example on all fours, with her back arched down, shoulders and butt raised with her legs slightly apart showing her very neat bulging pussy, that is what most men like to see. That one position revealing that bulge and the shape of a nice, round, firm butt surrounding the pussy is the biggest turn on for a man. Now that may not be the case for all men but it is the case for most. Men like to ask if you saw her pussy bulge see her pussy bulge, or they will be telling their holiday stories and will describe a woman's pussy, saying she was hanging well, she had big bulging lips just hanging down like curtains. lol Sorry; I did say it was a bit basic and sometimes I think that these things need to be said in a basic way as then it leaves no doubts and everyone understands.

Now SIZE; does it matter? Well let's deal with women first. Length matters more than width but not in the way that men need fear actually. The length and width of the average man is perfect for most women. Some women like long cocks but it is more uncomfortable for most women. Lots of them like fatter cocks but not too fat. In other words the average woman prefers the average cock, and if there was a choice most would choose wider over longer but let's not get stupid; anything over six inches in girth, which is all the way around, is getting uncomfortable for most woman. I am not saying that they cannot take much wider cocks because they can but only if aroused properly or well lubricated first. It's just that I have found that women feel comfortable with a cock that achieves what they need so it really is how you use it and all about the fore play and the picture you paint and how you go about enjoying each other.

Now for men. lol What is it with you all? Why are you all obsessed with the size of your cock? IT REALLY DOES NOT MATTER! For women who are less experienced than most let's start at the beginning. Some men have small cocks when soft or in other words not sexually excited. They can be two inches in length or even smaller but once aroused they can grow into a good five to six inches and more than double in girth when it is full of blood due to being sexually aroused. Other men have a cock that is, let's say, five inches soft and when full of blood and erect they are not much bigger at all; say a half inch to an inch longer and hardly any difference in girth. So don't judge a book by its cover, ladies, since a small soft cock is not always at its full potential whereas a fairly average five to six inches soft cock is probably near its full size.

Some men have been circumcised; in other words they've had some of the foreskin removed revealing their bell end which is the mushroom at the tip of the cock. lol Sorry, but some may not know this and you would be surprised to find out how many don't know the basics. Also some men who still have all their foreskin cannot pull the foreskin all the way back to reveal their bell end unless they are very wet, so it can be uncomfortable when putting their cocks into a tight or dry pussy. and I must say at this point that a man who still has his foreskin usually has more sensitivity in his bell end.

Some men have big ball bags and some have small ones and it does not necessarily go hand-in-hand that a big cock has a big ball bag, though some do. Lol Women like the feeling of a ball bag banging against their pussy when being taken from behind and a ball bag will swing better if it is warm. lol As the skin of the bag is very sensitive to heat it becomes almost elasticised. lol

Well I hope all that information was good for someone. lol If it helps one person to enjoy a better sex life then that's a bonus and as I said previously I have only put this in because I have talked to quite a few women who thought they were having good sex but due to lack of knowledge they actually were not. It is just that they did not know any better and had not experienced some things they might otherwise have which could be due to not communicating with their partner through embarrassment or lack of knowledge.

I have been reminded of a funny incident with one of my favourite people. One day we were talking about the colour of pussy pubes. lol Don't tell me you don't have these sort of conversations; everyone does, don't they? lol She asked what my favourite colour was and I tell her lol I like any colour but I do prefer black pubic hair, even though my wives were blondes. "I say wives like there was loads of them" and most of my sexual partners have been blonde so not a black pube in sight lol, well I have had partners with black hair and black pubes so I have at least had the vision lol and the experience. lol So Bike says, with a sideways glance and a twinkle in her eye, That she will get some hair dye and change the colour of her pubes for me and then she giggled obviously finding it very funny. Naturally I agreed that she should go for it and let me know when so I could help lol

Well it was not long, just a few days later, and she is around at my place and the subject came up again.

"So have you got the dye?" I asked "Yes" she giggled as she rummaged around in her handbag.

To my amazement she produced a can of spray hair dye. I can honestly say that I never knew it came in spray can form lol. Anyway we are both giggling like school girls as she sits on the toilet with her dress up around her waist and her panties around her ankles with me knelt in front of her shaking the can up and down like a can of paint, getting ready to do the spray job on her pussy. We are really laughing as I give it a quick squirt and it was really funny that I got it dead centre and just above the crack of her lips was a perfectly round black spot about the size of a two pound coin. I almost wet myself as I squirted the can and she sort of stiffened up and jumped back a little as if I had shot her. We were both still laughing a lot as I continued to spray. Now anyone who has had experience using a can of spray will know that it is best to mask off the area around the area to be sprayed to avoid a mess. Well I did not and by the time I had finished she had all the front of her pussy jet black as well as the top of her inner thighs and it was a right mess but oh so funny. I regret not taking before and after pictures so you could all see. I will do it again in the future but next time I will be more knowledgeable and get it right. It was great fun and I could see the sexy side as well as the funny side.

Well I am sitting here on my own tonight as my son is with his mother for the half term, and the most exciting thing I have lined up this week is DIY for Bike, fitting a new sliding wardrobe and laying a laminate floor and I am making a base and erecting an expensive shed in her mum's back garden. I have no dates. WHY?!! Well because I am not on any sites at the moment and have not got the money or the time.

My son living with me takes up a lot of my time and I would not swap this time for anything, even a beautiful woman. Honestly lol I have quality time with him every night and I have found that just going for a walk while he rides his scooter (the latest craze) lol turns out to be fantastic. He will open up and say things that I would have to coax out of him in other situations.

We walk for about a mile or so and it does seem like a long way but it is not really. He will start off talking about his scooter and stunts he is learning then he will ramble on about all the different upgrades you can get for it and all the information like the internet site, the price, the weight and how strong it is compared with other similar bits lol He is very thorough when he does research not sure where he gets that from. lol Definately not his mum. lol of course he's letting me know in his own way that this is what he wants for his next present, whether it be christmas or his birthday.

We have discussed his budget for Christmas lol Yes I know; a 10 year old discussing budgets. lol He has a bank account where I put his pocket money and his mum does as well so he is learning how valuable money is and how far it WONT go. lol

As I was saying, it's not long before he starts to talk about school and what he did at playtime, about individuals he plays with, incidents that happened in the playground and also in class. He is very bright and has many talents that I can see and I do my best to encourage what he is good at and also to experience new things. If you're no good at something what the heck because at least you've had a go. DON'T push your kids into doing what you want them to do because what they are good at naturally will come out in the end as long as you encourage them and you dont push them. I have found out that giving him the information and all the possible outcomes he will eventually come to a decision that usually sits well with the both of us.

Well that's it; well for now it is. I have loads of stuff to tell, not just about after the wife lol but my childhood and my experiences of life from the Army, from bankruptcy, from, a successful business; a whole host of experiences from my past and hopefully I will experience many more.

Maybe you will be in the next book. Lol there's still some to write about but I felt like it may be too repetitive and from my experience of reading which actually is very little a lot of books could be reduced by a third by taking out the continuous repeats I could have put in ambience and smells, colours and temperatures, but wanted to just paint a picture and let your imagination do the rest.

I hope this has been an interesting read. I apologise if I have any information incorrect or if I have shocked anyone but this is a true look at my life as it has happened in the last two years.

And Finally.

I want to add this because when I was low emotionally I was working for a very well known boat company. I had been employed by them working as a trainee laminator until I handed in my notice after eight months. This was for many reasons but mainly because my son was coming back to live with me and also because the job gave me tennis elbow, I had a lot to offer the company but they were very much stuck in the mode of you do as you're told.

I really hope they change their ways and survive this recession; not because I like them, but because of all the people that work there and the living they make out of working for them. When I left I went back to work for the previous company I had worked for as a contractor to the boat company and I had about a four week break before starting to work for the contractors who I will say were very good people. During this break I had picked up my son and we had a couple of weeks together during the summer holidays and my start back with this company coincided with my son starting school. It was a very well executed plan. lol I was there for a week and on the last day of the working week the HR manager walked into where I was working and asked me what I was doing there as I worked for them now,

No I left about four weeks ago I said with a smile, Then I explained the reasons why, as I told earlier. he nodded "that's a shame because you were knocking on our door to get a job with us".

Actually that was not the case as I had heard there were vacancies so I filled in an application the same as many others had done and they rang me and asked if I would like an interview. Anyway needless to say I was offered a job, but I did not say any of this to him as there was no real point. then he asked me what did you think of my time with them"? Well he did ask and I do tell it as it is so I told him I was actually disappointed and that I would only use an example that he was involved in as any other example could not be defended. I told him of the time when he was walking through the shop floor where I was working and that I had pointed out to him a safety issue where I was being asked to climb to my place of work with ten kg buckets of resin using pallets and that I was being told to work standing on this as a work platform. He had told me he would look into it immediately and get it sorted but in the meantime I should fill in a near miss, **he** said "I will look into this immediately and get it sorted but in the mean time could you fill in a near miss please" which I did. Now this had taken place three months before I left and from talking to people on the shop floor it seemed the norm that there was loads of, shall we say, LIP SERVICE BEING PAID but very little action. After I had reminded him about this and also pointed out that he had failed to follow up on it and that my near miss report had not been followed up on either and that there were many other issues that had needed addressing he seemed to get a little defensive.

Well not twenty four hours had passed before I get a phone call from my employer saying that this HR manager had contacted them and said that he did not want me on any of their sites again which left the company I worked for in a position where they had to sack me as their contracts were solely with this company. So there was a nose dive in emotions because as a single parent I was not able to get any benefits at that time I was not getting any maintenance either and I had just been sacked, I could have reported them to the HSE but I had thoughts of all those people out of work so MAYBE, MAYBE not.

So here I am with a very small amount of money in the bank, a small pension coming in that is not enough to cover all the bills, no job, no maintenance and no Jobseekers allowance. But I have now just got the first month's child benefit so it is a start and I won't be unemployed for long I have an interview tomorrow; it is only seventeen and a half hours a week cleaning but it means I will be able to claim tax credits etc so it's not all dismal and there is light at the end of this very long tunnel.

Now you know me, you know how I think, and what kind of person I am. Hopefully you will like me.

DAVE. Xx

UPDATE AUGUST 2012

My son and I are happy and enjoying life together, I am working as a supervisor for a cleaning company 30 hours a week, Hoping for success with this book and looking at writing another, probably more about me and my life BEFORE the wife lol and some stories that were not in this book.

Lifeafterthewife55@yahoo.com
Please feel free to contact me; I will reply if I can.